UPPER ROOM HYMNS

"And when they had sung a hymn, they went out into the Mount of Olives." Matthew 26:30

Compiled by
HARRY DENMAN
GROVER C. EMMONS

Music Editor
GEORGE SANVILLE

ISBN 0-687-43054-2

ABINGDON PRESS
Nashville ● *New York*

FOREWORD

"Enter into his gates with thanksgiving, and into his courts with praise: be thankful unto him, and bless his name."

It is the natural impulse of thankfulness, reverence, adoration, and faith to break forth into song. This accounts for the Book of Psalms and for the rich heritage of sacred music produced in the Christian era.

The purpose of this book is not only to meet the requirements for public worship, but also to preserve those hymns and songs which are rich in Christian experience and full of faith, hope, love, reverence, and loyalty, and which have therefore endeared themselves to devout worshipers in the past. With these have been included more recent songs that have won approval.

May this volume be found worthy and useful in the service of the Kingdom of Him who has brought joy, liberty, and song into the hearts of multitudes of his disciples.

CHARLES C. SELECMAN, *Chairman*
GENERAL COMMISSION ON EVANGELISM

1   Doxology

THOS. KEN   G. FRANC

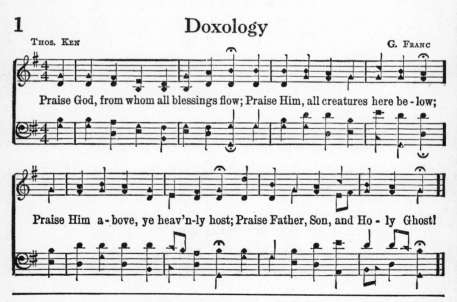

Praise God, from whom all blessings flow; Praise Him, all creatures here be-low;

Praise Him a-bove, ye heav'n-ly host; Praise Father, Son, and Ho-ly Ghost!

UPPER ROOM HYMNS

2   Guide Me, O Thou Great Jehovah

WILLIAM WILLIAMS

THOMAS HASTINGS

1. Guide me, O Thou great Je - ho - vah, Pil - grim thro' this bar - ren land; I am weak, but Thou art might - y, Hold me with Thy pow'r - ful hand; Bread of heav - en, Feed me till I want no more; Bread of heav - en, Feed me till I want no more.

2. O - pen now the crys - tal foun - tain Whence the heal - ing wa - ters flow; Let the fi - er - y, cloud - y pil - lar Lead me all my jour - ney thro'; Strong De - liv - 'rer, Be Thou still my Strength and Shield; Strong De - liv - 'rer, Be Thou still my Strength and Shield.

3. When I tread the verge of Jor - dan, Bid my anx - ious fears sub - side; Bear me thro' the swell - ing cur - rent, Land me safe on Ca - naan's side: Songs of prais - es I will ev - er give to Thee; Songs of prais - es I will ev - er give to Thee.

3   All Hail the Power of Jesus' Name

EDWARD PERRONET   OLIVER HOLDEN

1. All hail the pow'r of Je-sus' name, Let an-gels pros-trate fall;
2. Crown Him, ye morn-ing stars of light, Who fixed this earth-ly ball;
3. Sin-ners, whose love can ne'er for-get The wormwood and the gall,
4. Let ev-'ry kin-dred, ev-'ry tribe, On this ter-res-trial ball,
5. O that with yon-der sa-cred throng We at His feet may fall;

Bring forth the roy-al di-a-dem, And crown Him Lord of all,
Now hail the strength of Is-rael's might, And crown Him Lord of all,
Go, spread your tro-phies at His feet, And crown Him Lord of all,
To Him all maj-es-ty as-cribe, And crown Him Lord of all,
We'll join the ev-er-last-ing song, And crown Him Lord of all,

Bring forth the roy-al di-a-dem, And crown Him Lord of all.
Now hail the strength of Is-rael's might, And crown Him Lord of all.
Go, spread your tro-phies at His feet, And crown Him Lord of all.
To Him all maj-es-ty as-cribe, And crown Him Lord of all.
We'll join the ev-er-last-ing song, And crown Him Lord of all.

4   Blest Be the Tie

JOHN FAWCETT   HANS G. NAEGELI

1. Blest be the tie that binds Our hearts in Chris-tian love; The
2. Be-fore our Fa-ther's throne, We pour our ar-dent prayers; Our
3. We share our mu-tual woes, Our mu-tual bur-dens bear; And
4. When we a-sun-der part, It gives us in-ward pain; But

Blest Be the Tie

fel - low - ship of kin - dred minds Is like to that a - bove.
fears, our hopes, our aims are one, Our com - forts and our cares.
oft - en for each oth - er flows The sym - pa - thiz - ing tear.
we shall still be joined in heart, And hope to meet a - gain.

5   There Is a Fountain

WILLIAM COWPER   LOWELL MASON

1. There is a foun-tain filled with blood Drawn from Im - man - uel's veins;
2. The dy - ing thief re - joiced to see That foun - tain in his day;
3. Dear dy - ing Lamb, Thy pre-cious blood Shall nev - er lose its pow'r,
4. E'er since, by faith, I saw the stream Thy flow - ing wounds sup - ply,
5. Then in a no - bler, sweet-er song, I'll sing Thy pow'r to save,

D.S.-And sin-ners, plunged be-neath that flood, Lose all their guilt - y stains.
D.S.-And there may I, though vile as he, Wash all my sins a - way.
D.S.-Till all the ran-somed church of God Be saved, to sin no more.
D.S.-Re - deem-ing love has been my theme, And shall be till I die.
D.S.-When this poor lisp-ing, stamm'ring tongue Lies si - lent in the grave.

FINE

D. S.

Lose all their guilt - y stains,   Lose all their guilt - y stains;
Wash all my sins a - way,   Wash all my sins a - way;
Be saved, to sin no more,   Be saved, to sin no more;
And shall be till I die,   And shall be till I die;
Lies si - lent in the grave,   Lies si - lent in the grave;

6 In the Cross of Christ

Sir John Bowring

Ithamar Conkey

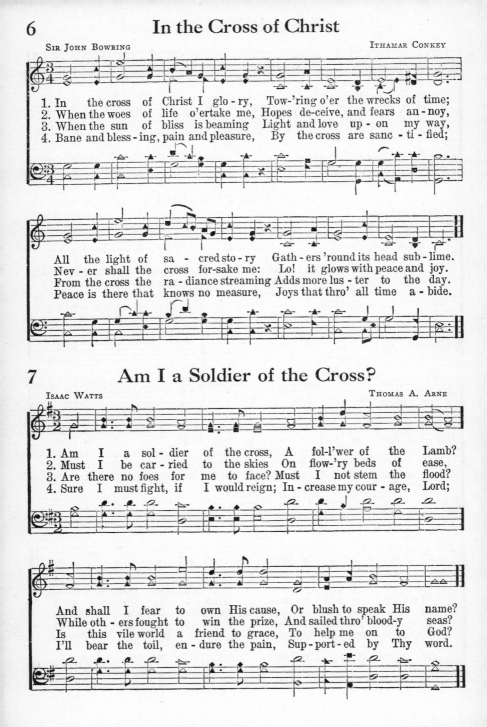

1. In the cross of Christ I glo - ry, Tow-'ring o'er the wrecks of time;
2. When the woes of life o'ertake me, Hopes de-ceive, and fears an - noy,
3. When the sun of bliss is beaming Light and love up - on my way,
4. Bane and bless - ing, pain and pleasure, By the cross are sanc - ti - fied;

All the light of sa - cred sto - ry Gath - ers 'round its head sub - lime.
Nev - er shall the cross for-sake me: Lo! it glows with peace and joy.
From the cross the ra - diance streaming Adds more lus - ter to the day.
Peace is there that knows no measure, Joys that thro' all time a - bide.

7 Am I a Soldier of the Cross?

Isaac Watts

Thomas A. Arne

1. Am I a sol - dier of the cross, A fol-l'wer of the Lamb?
2. Must I be car - ried to the skies On flow-'ry beds of ease,
3. Are there no foes for me to face? Must I not stem the flood?
4. Sure I must fight, if I would reign; In - crease my cour - age, Lord;

And shall I fear to own His cause, Or blush to speak His name?
While oth - ers fought to win the prize, And sailed thro' blood-y seas?
Is this vile world a friend to grace, To help me on to God?
I'll bear the toil, en - dure the pain, Sup - port - ed by Thy word.

8 Onward, Christian Soldiers

Sabine Baring-Gould

Arthur Sullivan

1. On-ward, Christian sol - diers! Marching as to war, With the cross of
2. Like a might-y ar - my Moves the Church of God; Brothers, we are
3. Crowns and thrones may per-ish, Kingdoms rise and wane; But the Church of
4. On-ward, then, ye peo - ple! Join our happy throng; Blend with ours your

Je - sus Go - ing on be - fore; Christ, the roy - al Mas - ter,
tread - ing Where the saints have trod; We are not di - vid - ed,
Je - sus Con-stant will re - main; Gates of hell can nev - er
voic - es In the tri-umph song; Glo - ry, laud, and hon - or,

Leads a-gainst the foe; For-ward in - to bat - tle, See, His banners go!
All one bod - y we; One in hope and doc - trine, One in char - i - ty.
'Gainst that Church prevail; We have Christ's own promise, Which can never fail.
Un - to Christ the King; This thro' countless a - ges Men and an - gels sing.

CHORUS

On-ward, Chris-tian sol - diers! March-ing as to war,

With the cross of Je - sus Go - ing on be - fore.

9 Faith of Our Fathers

Frederick W. Faber

H. F. Hemy

1. Faith of our fa-thers! liv-ing still In spite of dun-geon, fire and sword:
2. Our fa-thers, chained in prisons dark, Were still in heart and conscience free:
3. Faith of our fa-thers! we will love Both friend and foe in all our strife:

O how our hearts beat high with joy Whene'er we hear that glo-rious word
How sweet would be their children's fate, If they, like them, could die for thee!
And preach thee, too, as love knows how, By kind-ly words and vir-tuous life:

Faith of our fa-thers! ho-ly faith! We will be true to thee till death!
Faith of our fa-thers! ho-ly faith! We will be true to thee till death!
Faith of our fa-thers! ho-ly faith! We will be true to thee till death!

10 Holy Ghost, With Light Divine

A. Reed

Gottschalk

1. Ho-ly Ghost, with light di-vine, Shine up-on this heart of mine;
2. Ho-ly Ghost, with pow'r di-vine, Cleanse this guilt-y heart of mine;
3. Ho-ly Ghost, with joy di-vine, Cheer this saddened heart of mine;
4. Ho-ly Spir-it, all di-vine, Dwell with-in this heart of mine;

Holy Ghost, With Light Divine

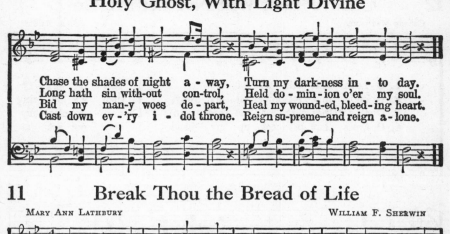

Chase the shades of night a - way, Turn my dark-ness in - to day.
Long hath sin with-out con-trol, Held do - min - ion o'er my soul.
Bid my man-y woes de - part, Heal my wound-ed, bleed-ing heart.
Cast down ev - 'ry i - dol throne. Reign su-preme—and reign a - lone.

11 Break Thou the Bread of Life

MARY ANN LATHBURY   WILLIAM F. SHERWIN

1. Break Thou the bread of life, Dear Lord, to me, As Thou didst
2. Bless Thou the truth, dear Lord, To me—to me— As Thou didst
3. O send Thy Spir - it, Lord, Now un - to me, That He may
4. Thou art the bread of life, O Lord, to me, Thy ho - ly

break the loaves Be - side the sea; Be - yond the sa - cred page
bless the bread By Gal - i - lee; Then shall all bond - age cease,
touch my eyes, And make me see: Show me the truth con-cealed
Word the truth That sav - eth me; Give me to eat and live

I seek Thee, Lord; My spir - it pants for Thee, O liv - ing Word.
All fet - ters fall; And I shall find my peace, My All in all.
With - in Thy Word, And in Thy book re-vealed I see the Lord.
With Thee a - bove; Teach me to love Thy truth, For Thou art love.

12 O Love That Wilt Not Let Me Go

GEORGE MATHESON

A. L. PEACE

1. O Love that wilt not let me go, I rest my wea - ry
2. O Light that fol - low'st all my way, I yield my flick - 'ring
3. O Joy that seek - est me thro' pain, I can - not close my
4. O Cross that lift - est up my head, I dare not ask to

soul in Thee; I give Thee back the life I owe, That
torch to Thee; My heart re - stores its bor - rowed ray, That
heart to Thee; I trace the rain - bow thro' the rain, And
hide from Thee; I lay in dust life's glo - ry dead, And

in Thine o - cean depths its flow May rich - er, full - er be.
in Thy sun-shine's glow its day May bright - er, fair - er be.
feel the prom - ise is not vain That morn shall tear - less be.
from the ground there blossoms red Life that shall end - less be.

13 On Jordan's Stormy Banks

SAMUEL STENNETT

Arr. by R. M. McINTOSH

1. On Jor - dan's stormy banks I stand, And cast a wish - ful eye
2. All o'er those wide, ex - tend - ed plains Shines one e - ter - nal day;
3. No chill - ing winds, nor pois'nous breath, Can reach that healthful shore;
4. When shall I reach that hap - py place, And be for - ev - er blest?

On Jordan's Stormy Banks

To Ca-naan's fair and hap-py land, Where my pos-ses-sions lie.
There God, the Son, for-ev-er reigns, And scat-ters night a-way.
Sick-ness and sor-row, pain and death, Are felt and feared no more.
When shall I see my Fa-ther's face, And in His bos-om rest?

D. S.—*O who will come and go with me? I am bound for the promised land.*

REFRAIN

I am bound for the promised land,...... I am bound for the promised land.
promised land,

14 Come, Thou Fount

ROBERT ROBINSON

JOHN WYETH

1. { Come, Thou Fount of ev-'ry bless-ing, Tune my heart to sing Thy grace;
     Streams of mer-cy, nev-er ceas-ing, Call for songs of loud-est praise. }

2. { Here I'll raise my Eb-en-e-zer, Hith-er by Thy help I'll come;
     And I hope, by Thy good pleasure, Safe-ly to ar-rive at home. }

3. { Oh, to grace How great a debt-or Dai-ly I'm constrained to be!
     Let Thy good-ness, like a fet-ter, Bind my wand'-ring heart to Thee: }

D.C.—Praise the mount, I'm fixed up-on it! Mount of Thy re-deem-ing love.
D.C.—He, to res-cue me from dan-ger, In-ter-posed His pre-cious blood.
D.C.—Here's my heart, O take and seal it, Seal it for Thy courts a-bove.

Teach me some me-lo-dious son-net, Sung by flam-ing tongues a-bove;
Je-sus sought me when a stran-ger, Wand'ring from the fold of God;
Prone to wan-der, Lord, I feel it, Prone to leave the God I love;

15 I Walk With the King

JAMES ROWE

B. D. ACKLEY

1. In sor-row I wan-dered, my spir-it op-prest, But now I am
2. For years in the fet-ters of sin I was bound, The world could not
3. O soul near de-spair in the low-lands of strife, Look up and let

hap-py—se-cure-ly I rest; From morn-ing till eve-ning glad
help me—no com-fort I found; But now like the birds and the
Je-sus come in-to your life; The joy of sal-va-tion to

car-ols I sing, And this is the rea-son—I walk with the King.
sunbeams of spring, I'm free and re-joic-ing—I walk with the King.
you He would bring—Come in-to the sun-light and walk with the King.

CHORUS

I walk with the King, hal-le-lu-jah! I walk with the King, praise His name!

No lon-ger I roam, my soul fa-ces home, I walk and I talk with the King.

16 Savior, Like a Shepherd Lead Us

DOROTHY ANN THRUPP

WILLIAM B. BRADBURY

1. Sav - ior, like a Shep-herd lead us, Much we need Thy ten-der care;
2. We are Thine, do Thou be - friend us, Be the Guardian of our way;
3. Thou hast promised to re - ceive us, Poor and sin-ful tho' we be;
4. Ear - ly let us seek Thy fa - vor; Ear - ly let us seek Thy will;

In Thy pleasant pas-tures feed us, For our use Thy folds pre-pare:
Keep Thy flock, from sin de - fend us, Seek us when we go a-stray:
Thou hast mer-cy to re - lieve us, Grace to cleanse, and pow'r to free:
Bless - ed Lord and on - ly Sav - ior, With Thy love our bos-oms fill:

Bless-ed Je - sus, Bless-ed Je - sus, Thou hast bought us, Thine we are;
Bless-ed Je - sus, Bless-ed Je - sus, Hear Thy chil-dren when they pray;
Bless-ed Je - sus, Bless-ed Je - sus, Ear-ly let us turn to Thee;
Bless-ed Je - sus, Bless-ed Je - sus, Thou hast loved us, love us still;

Bless-ed Je - sus, Bless-ed Je - sus, Thou hast bought us, Thine we are.
Bless-ed Je - sus, Bless-ed Je - sus, Hear Thy children when they pray.
Bless-ed Je - sus, Bless-ed Je - sus, Ear-ly let us turn to Thee.
Bless-ed Je - sus, Bless-ed Je - sus, Thou hast loved us, love us still.

17 Amazing Grace

JOHN NEWTON

1. A - maz-ing grace! how sweet the sound, That saved a wretch like me! I
2. 'Twas grace that taught my heart to fear, And grace my fears re-lieved; How
3. Thro' man - y dan-gers, toils and snares, I have al - read - y come; 'Tis
4. When we've been there ten thousand years, Bright shining as the sun, We've

once was lost, but now am found, Was blind, but now I see.
pre - cious did that grace ap-pear The hour I first be-lieved!
grace hath bro't me safe thus far, And grace will lead me home.
no less days to sing God's praise Than when we first be - gun. A-men.

18 Holy, Holy, Holy

REGINALD HEBER

REV. JOHN B. DYKES

1. Ho - ly, Ho - ly, Ho - ly, Lord God Al-might - y! Ear - ly in the
2. Ho - ly, Ho - ly, Ho - ly! All the saints a - dore Thee, Cast-ing down their
3. Ho - ly, Ho - ly, Ho - ly! Tho' the darkness hide Thee, Tho' the eye of
4. Ho - ly, Ho - ly, Ho - ly, Lord God Al-might - y! All Thy works shall

morn - ing our song shall rise to Thee; Ho - ly, Ho - ly, Ho - ly!
golden crowns a - round the glass - y sea; Cher - u - bim and ser-a-phim
sin - ful man Thy glo - ry may not see, On - ly Thou art ho - ly;
praise Thy name in earth, and sky, and sea; Ho - ly, Ho - ly, Ho - ly!

Holy, Holy, Holy

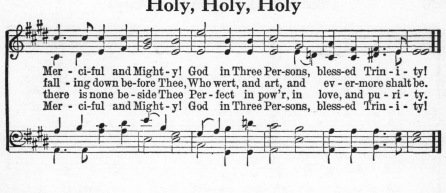

Mer - ci-ful and Might - y! God in Three Per-sons, bless-ed Trin - i - ty!
fall - ing down be-fore Thee, Who wert, and art, and ev - er-more shalt be.
there is none be - side Thee Per - fect in pow'r, in love, and pu - ri - ty.
Mer - ci-ful and Might - y! God in Three Per-sons, bless-ed Trin - i - ty!

19 Rock of Ages

Augustus M. Toplady

Thomas Hastings

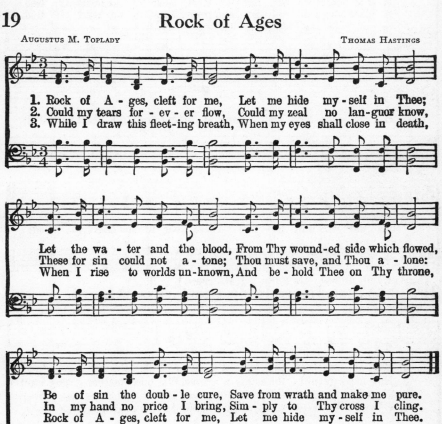

1. Rock of A - ges, cleft for me, Let me hide my - self in Thee;
2. Could my tears for - ev - er flow, Could my zeal no lan-guor know,
3. While I draw this fleet-ing breath, When my eyes shall close in death,

Let the wa - ter and the blood, From Thy wound-ed side which flowed,
These for sin could not a - tone; Thou must save, and Thou a - lone:
When I rise to worlds un-known, And be - hold Thee on Thy throne,

Be of sin the doub - le cure, Save from wrath and make me pure.
In my hand no price I bring, Sim - ply to Thy cross I cling.
Rock of A - ges, cleft for me, Let me hide my - self in Thee.

20 Near to the Heart of God

C. B. McAfee

1. There is a place of qui-et rest, Near to the heart of God,
2. There is a place of com-fort sweet, Near to the heart of God,
3. There is a place of full re-lease, Near to the heart of God,

A place where sin can-not mo-lest, Near to the heart of God.
A place where we our Sav-ior meet, Near to the heart of God.
A place where all is joy and peace, Near to the heart of God.

REFRAIN

O Je-sus, blest Re-deem-er, Sent from the heart of God,

Hold us, who wait be-fore Thee, Near to the heart of God.

21 Must Jesus Bear the Cross Alone?

THOS. SHEPHERD   GEO. N. ALLEN

1. Must Je-sus bear the cross a-lone, And all the world go free?
2. How hap-py are the saints a-bove, Who once went sor-rowing here!
3. The con-se-cra-ted cross I'll bear, Till death shall set me free;
4. Up-on the crys-tal pave-ment, down, At Je-sus' pierc-ed feet,

Must Jesus Bear the Cross Alone?

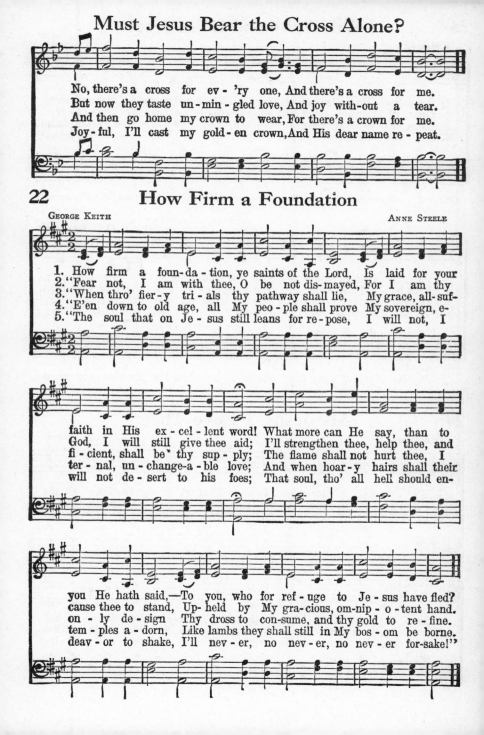

No, there's a cross for ev - 'ry one, And there's a cross for me.
But now they taste un - min - gled love, And joy with-out a tear.
And then go home my crown to wear, For there's a crown for me.
Joy - ful, I'll cast my gold - en crown, And His dear name re - peat.

22 How Firm a Foundation

GEORGE KEITH

ANNE STEELE

1. How firm a foun - da - tion, ye saints of the Lord, Is laid for your
2. "Fear not, I am with thee, O be not dis-mayed, For I am thy
3. "When thro' fier-y tri - als thy pathway shall lie, My grace, all-suf-
4. "E'en down to old age, all My peo - ple shall prove My sovereign, e-
5. "The soul that on Je - sus still leans for re - pose, I will not, I

faith in His ex - cel - lent word! What more can He say, than to
God, I will still give thee aid; I'll strengthen thee, help thee, and
fi - cient, shall be thy sup - ply; The flame shall not hurt thee, I
ter - nal, un - change-a - ble love; And when hoar-y hairs shall their
will not de - sert to his foes; That soul, tho' all hell should en-

you He hath said,—To you, who for ref - uge to Je - sus have fled?
cause thee to stand, Up- held by My gra - cious, om-nip - o - tent hand.
on - ly de - sign Thy dross to con-sume, and thy gold to re - fine.
tem - ples a - dorn, Like lambs they shall still in My bos - om be borne.
deav - or to shake, I'll nev - er, no nev - er, no nev - er for-sake!"

23 I Will Arise and Go to Jesus

J. HART

Arranged

1. Come, ye sin-ners, poor and need-y, Weak and wound-ed, sick and sore;
2. Come, ye thirst-y, come, and welcome, God's free boun-ty glo - ri - fy;
3. Come, ye wea - ry, heav-y - la - den, Lost and ru - ined by the fall;
4. Let not conscience make you lin - ger, Nor of fit - ness fond-ly dream;

CHO.—*I will a-rise and go to Je - sus, He will em-brace me in His arms;*

D. C. for Chorus

Je - sus read-y stands to save you, Full of pit - y, love and pow'r.
True be - lief and true re - pent-ance, Ev - 'ry grace that brings you nigh.
If you tar - ry till you're bet - ter, You will nev - er come at all.
All the fit - ness He re - quir-eth Is to feel your need of Him.

In the arms of my dear Sav - ior, Oh, there are ten thou-sand charms.

24 My Jesus, I Love Thee

ANONYMOUS

A. J. GORDON

1. My Je - sus, I love Thee, I know Thou art mine, For Thee all the
2. I'll love Thee in life, I will love Thee in death, And praise Thee as
3. In mansions of glo - ry and end - less de - light, I'll ev - er a -

fol - lies of sin I re - sign; My gra - cious Re - deem - er, my
long as Thou lend - est me breath; And say when the death-dew lies
dore Thee in heav - en so bright; I'll sing with the glit - ter - ing

My Jesus, I Love Thee

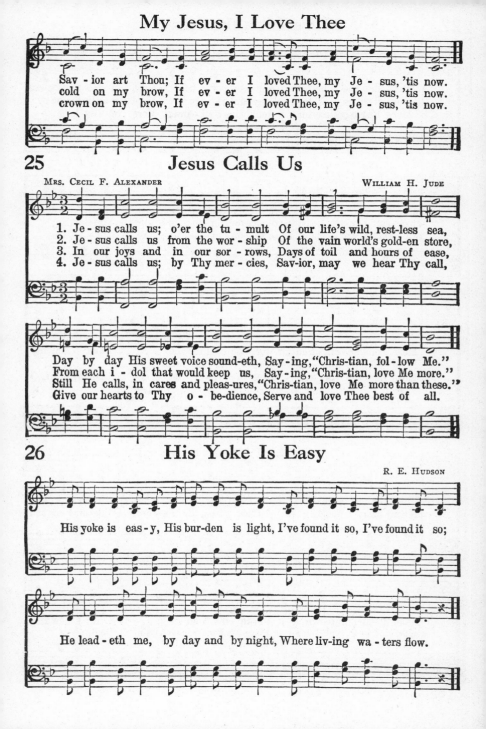

Sav - ior art Thou; If ev - er I loved Thee, my Je - sus, 'tis now.
cold on my brow, If ev - er I loved Thee, my Je - sus, 'tis now.
crown on my brow, If ev - er I loved Thee, my Je - sus, 'tis now.

25 Jesus Calls Us

MRS. CECIL F. ALEXANDER

WILLIAM H. JUDE

1. Je - sus calls us; o'er the tu - mult Of our life's wild, rest-less sea,
2. Je - sus calls us from the wor - ship Of the vain world's gold-en store,
3. In our joys and in our sor - rows, Days of toil and hours of ease,
4. Je - sus calls us; by Thy mer - cies, Sav-ior, may we hear Thy call,

Day by day His sweet voice sound-eth, Say-ing, "Chris-tian, fol-low Me."
From each i - dol that would keep us, Say-ing, "Chris-tian, love Me more."
Still He calls, in cares and pleas-ures, "Chris-tian, love Me more than these."
Give our hearts to Thy o - be-dience, Serve and love Thee best of all.

26 His Yoke Is Easy

R. E. HUDSON

His yoke is eas - y, His bur-den is light, I've found it so, I've found it so;

He lead - eth me, by day and by night, Where liv-ing wa - ters flow.

27 More Like the Master

C. H. G.

CHAS. H. GABRIEL

1. More like the Mas-ter I would ev - er be, More of His meek-ness,
2. More like the Mas-ter is my dai - ly prayer; More strength to car-ry
3. More like the Mas-ter I would live and grow; More of His love to

more hu - mil - i - ty; More zeal to la - bor, more cour-age to be true,
cross-es I must bear; More ear-nest ef - fort to bring His kingdom in;
oth - ers I would show; More self-de - ni - al, like His in Gal - i - lee,

rit.

CHORUS.

More con - se - cra - tion for work He bids me do. . . . . . Take Thou my
More of His Spir - it, the wan-der - er to win. . . . .
More like the Mas-ter I long to ev - er be. . . . . Take my heart, O

heart, . . I would be Thine a-lone; . . Take Thou my heart . . and
take my heart, I would be Thine a-lone; Take my heart, O take my heart and

make it all Thine own; . . Purge me from sin, . . . O Lord, I now im-
make it all Thine own; Purge Thou me from ev'ry sin, O Lord, I

More Like the Master

plore,.... Wash   me and keep.... me Thine for-ev - er - more.
now im-plore, Wash and keep, O wash and keep me Thine for-ev - er - more.

28   Fill Me Now

E. H. STOKES   JNO. R. SWENEY

1. Hov - er o'er me, Ho - ly Spir - it, Bathe my trembling heart and brow;
2. Thou canst fill me, gra-cious Spir - it, Though I can - not tell Thee how;
3. I   am weakness, full of weak - ness, At Thy sa - cred feet I bow;
4. Cleanse and comfort, bless and save me, Bathe, O bathe my heart and brow;

FINE

Fill   me with Thy hal-lowed pre-sence, Come, O come, and fill   me now.
But   I need Thee, greatly need Thee, Come, O come, and fill   me now.
Blest, di - vine, e - ter - nal Spir - it, Fill with pow'r, and fill   me now.
Thou art com-fort - ing and sav - ing, Thou art sweet - ly fill - ing now.

D. S.–*Fill me with Thy hal-lowed presence, Come, O come, and fill me now.*

REFRAIN   D. S.

Fill me now, fill   me now,   Je - sus, come, and fill   me now;

Have Thine Own Way, Lord

A. A. P.

Geo. C. Stebbins

Slowly

1. Have Thine own way, Lord! Have Thine own way!.. Thou art the
2. Have Thine own way, Lord! Have Thine own way!.. Search me and
3. Have Thine own way, Lord! Have Thine own way!.. Wound-ed and
4. Have Thine own way, Lord! Have Thine own way!.. Hold o'er my

Pot - ter; I am the clay... Mould me and make me Aft - er Thy
try me, Mas-ter, to - day!... Whit - er than snow, Lord, Wash me just
wea - ry, Help me, I pray!. Pow - er—all pow - er—Sure - ly is
be - ing Ab - so - lute sway!. Fill with Thy Spir - it Till all shall

will,... While I am wait - ing, Yield - ed and still...
now,... As in Thy pres - ence Hum - bly I bow...
Thine! Touch me and heal me, Sav - ior di - vine!..
see.... Christ on - ly, al - ways, Liv - ing in me!....

My Faith Looks Up to Thee

Ray Palmer

Lowell Mason

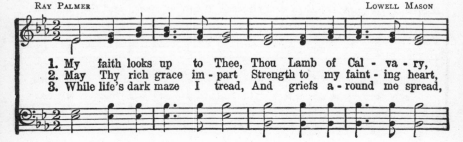

1. My faith looks up to Thee, Thou Lamb of Cal - va - ry,
2. May Thy rich grace im - part Strength to my faint - ing heart,
3. While life's dark maze I tread, And griefs a - round me spread,

My Faith Looks Up to Thee

Sav - ior di - vine; Now hear me when I pray, Take all my
My zeal in - spire; As Thou hast died for me, O may my
Be Thou my Guide; Bid dark - ness turn to day, Wipe sor - row's

sin a - way, O let me from this day Be whol - ly Thine!
love to Thee, Pure, warm, and changeless be,—A liv - ing fire!
tears a - way, Nor let me ev - er stray From Thee a - side.

31   O Happy Day

PHILIP DODDRIDGE   E. F. RIMBAULT

1. {O hap - py day that fixed my choice On Thee, my Sav - ior and my God! }
{Well may this glow-ing heart re - joice, And tell its rap - tures all a - broad.}
2. {O hap - py bond, that seals my vows To Him who mer - its all my love! }
{Let cheer - ful an - thems fill His house, While to that sa - cred shrine I move.}
3. {'Tis done: the great trans-ac-tion's done; I am my Lord's, and He is mine; }
{He drew me, and I fol-lowed on, Charmed to confess the voice di - vine. }
4. {Now rest, my long-di - vid - ed heart; Fixed on this bliss - ful cen - tre, rest; }
{Nor ev - er from my Lord de - part, With Him of ev - 'ry good possessed. }

FINE

Hap - py day, hap - py day, When Je - sus washed my sins a - way!

D. S.

He taught me how to watch and pray, And live re - joic - ing ev - 'ry day;

32

At the Cross

Isaac Watts

R. E. Hudson

1. {A - las! and did my Sav - ior bleed? And did my Sov - 'reign die?
    {Would He de - vote that sa - (Omit . . . .)
2. {Was it for crimes that I have done, He groaned up - on the tree?
    {A - maz - ing pit - y! grace (Omit . . . .)

cred head For such a worm as I?
un-known! And love be - yond de-gree! At the cross, at the cross, where I

first saw the light, And the burden of my heart rolled away, (rolled away,) It was

there by faith I re-ceived my sight, And now I am happy all the day.

33

Where He Leads Me

E. W. Blandly

J. S. Norris

1. I can hear my Sav - ior call - ing, I can hear my Sav - ior call - ing,
2. I'll go with Him thro' the gar - den, I'll go with Him thro' the gar - den,
3. I'll go with Him thro' the judg-ment, I'll go with Him thro' the judg-ment,
4. He will give me grace and glo - ry, He will give me grace and glo - ry,

Ref.—*Where He leads me I will fol - low, Where He leads me I will fol - low,*

Where He Leads Me

I can hear my Sav-ior call-ing, "Take thy cross and fol-low, fol-low Me."
I'll go with Him thro' the gar-den, I'll go with Him, with Him all the way.
I'll go with Him thro' the judg-ment, I'll go with Him, with Him all the way.
He will give me grace and glo-ry, And go with me, with me all the way.

Where He leads me I will fol-low, I'll go with Him, with Him all the way.

34 Something for Jesus

S. D. PHELPS

ROBERT LOWRY

1. Sav-ior, Thy dy-ing love Thou gav-est me, Nor should I
2. At the blest mer-cy-seat, Plead-ing for me, My fee-ble
3. Give me a faith-ful heart,—Like-ness to Thee,—That each de-
4. All that I am and have,—Thy gifts so free,— In joy, in

aught with-hold, Dear Lord, from Thee: In love my soul would bow, My heart ful-
faith looks up, Je-sus, to Thee: Help me the cross to bear, Thy wondrous
part-ing day Henceforth may see Some work of love be-gun, Some deed of
grief, thro' life, Dear Lord, for Thee! And when Thy face I see, My ransomed

fill its vow, Some of-f'ring bring Thee now, Something for Thee.
love de-clare, Some song to raise, or pray'r, Something for Thee.
kind-ness done, Some wand'rer sought and won, Something for Thee.
soul shall be, Thro' all e-ter-ni-ty, Something for Thee.

35 If Jesus Goes With Me

C. A. M.

C. Austin Miles

1. It may be in the val-ley, where countless dangers hide; It may be in the
2. It may be I must car - ry the bless- ed word of life A-cross the burning
3. But if it be my por- tion to bear my cross at home, While others bear their
4. It is not mine to ques-tion the judg-ments of my Lord, It is but mine to

sun - shine that I, in peace, a - bide; But this one thing I know—if
des - erts to those in sin - ful strife; And tho' it be my lot to
bur - dens be-yond the bil - low's foam, I'll prove my faith in Him—con-
fol - low the lead-ings of His Word; But if to go or stay, or

it be dark or fair, If Je - sus is with me, I'll go an - y - where!
bear my col - ors there, If Je - sus goes with me, I'll go an - y - where!
fess His judgments fair, And, if He stays with me, I'll stay an - y - where!
wheth-er here or there, I'll be, with my Sav - ior, Con-tent an - y - where!

CHORUS

If Je-sus goes with me, I'll go.... An - y - where! 'Tis heaven to me, Wher-
I'll go

e'er I may be, If He is there! I count it a priv - i - lege here.. His
His cross, His

Copyright, 1936, Renewal. Rodeheaver Co., owner.

If Jesus Goes With Me

cross to bear;.. If Je-sus goes with me, I'll go... An - y - where!
cross, His cross to bear;

36   Wonderful Words of Life

P. P. B.

P. P. Bliss

1. Sing them o - ver a - gain to me, Won-der - ful words of Life;
2. Christ, the bless - ed One, gives to all, Won-der - ful words of Life;
3. Sweet - ly ech - o the gos - pel call, Won-der - ful words of Life;

Let me more of their beau - ty see, Won-der - ful words of Life.
Sin - ner, list to the lov - ing call, Won-der - ful words of Life.
Of - fer par - don and peace to all, Won-der - ful words of Life.

Words of life and beau - ty, Teach me faith and du - ty,
All so free - ly giv - en, Woo - ing us to heav - en:
Je - sus, on - ly Sav - ior, Sanc - ti - fy for - ev - er:

REFRAIN   1   2

Beau-ti-ful words, won-der-ful words, Won-der - ful words of Life. Life.

Sunrise

37

W. C. POOLE

B. D. ACKLEY

SOLO

1. When I shall come to the end of my way, When I shall rest at the
2. When in His beau-ty I see the great King, Join with the ran-somed His
3. When life is o - ver and day-light is passed, In heav-en's har - bor my

close of life's day, When "Wel-come home" I shall hear Je - sus say, O
prais - es to sing, When I shall join them my trib - utes to bring, O
an - chor is cast, When I see Je - sus my Sav - ior at last, O

CHORUS

that will be sun-rise for me. . . . . Sun-rise to-mor-row, sun-rise to-

mor-row, Sun-rise in glo-ry is wait-ing for me; Sun-rise to-mor-row,

sun-rise to-mor-row, Sun-rise with Je-sus for e-ter-ni-ty.

38 There Is Glory in My Soul

Grace Weiser Davis   Chas. H. Gabriel

1. Since I lost my sins and I found my Sav-ior, There is glo-ry in my soul!
2. Since He cleansed my heart, gave me sight for blindness, There is glo-ry in my soul!
3. Since with God I've walked, having sweet communion, There is glo-ry in my soul!
4. Since I entered Canaan on my way to heav-en, There is glo-ry in my soul!

Since by faith I sought and obtained God's fa-vor, There is glo-ry in my soul!
Since He touched and healed me in loving kindness, There is glo-ry in my soul!
Brighter grows each day in this heav'nly un-ion, There is glo-ry in my soul!
Since the day my life to the Lord was giv-en, There is glo-ry in my soul!

Chorus

There is glo-ry, glo-ry, there is glo-ry in my soul! Ev-'ry day brighter grows, And I con-quer all my foes; There is glo-ry, glo-ry, there is glo-ry in my soul! There is glo-ry in my soul! glo-ry in my soul!

39 He Lives

A. H. A.   Rev. A. H. Ackley

1. I serve a ris-en Sav-ior, He's in the world to-day; I know that He is
2. In all the world a-round me I see His lov-ing care, And tho' my heart grows
3. Re-joice, re-joice, O Christian, lift up your voice and sing E - ter - nal hal - le-

liv - ing, what-ev - er men may say; I see His hand of mer - cy, I
wea - ry I nev - er will de-spair; I know that He is lead-ing, thro'
lu - jahs to Je - sus Christ the King! The Hope of all who seek Him, the

hear His voice of cheer, And just the time I need Him He's al-ways near.
all the storm-y blast, The day of His ap-pear-ing will come at last.
Help of all who find, None oth-er is so lov-ing, so good and kind.

Refrain *Spirited*

He lives, He lives, Christ Je-sus lives to - day! He walks with me and
He lives, He lives,

talks with me a-long life's nar-row way. He lives, He lives, sal-
He lives, He lives,

He Lives

rit. ff

va-tion to im - part! You ask me how I know He lives? He lives within my heart.

40 'Tis So Sweet to Trust in Jesus

LOUISA M. R. STEAD

WM. J. KIRKPATRICK

1. 'Tis so sweet to trust in Je - sus, Just to take Him at His Word;
2. O how sweet to trust in Je - sus, Just to trust His cleans-ing blood;
3. Yes, 'tis sweet to trust in Je - sus, Just from sin and self to cease;
4. I'm so glad I learned to trust Thee, Pre - cious Je - sus, Sav - ior, Friend;

Just to rest up - on His prom-ise; Just to know, "Thus saith the Lord."
Just in sim - ple faith to plunge me 'Neath the heal-ing, cleans-ing flood!
Just from Je - sus sim - ply tak-ing Life and rest, and joy and peace.
And I know that Thou art with me, Wilt be with me to the end.

CHORUS

Je - sus, Je - sus, how I trust Him! How I've proved Him o'er and o'er!

p

Je - sus, Je - sus, pre - cious Je - sus! O for grace to trust Him more!

41 Pentecostal Power

Charlotte G. Homer

Chas. H. Gabriel

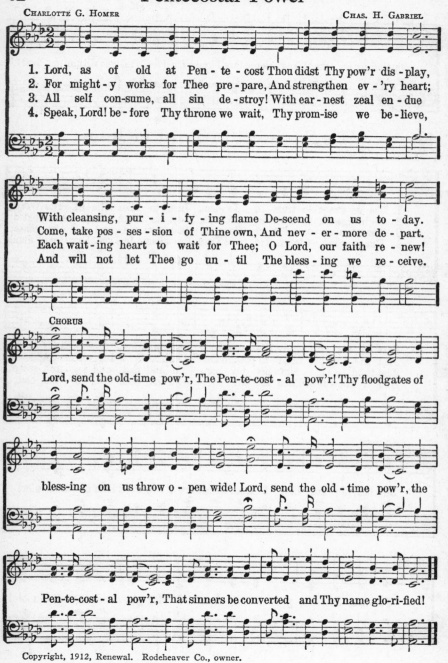

1. Lord, as of old at Pen - te - cost Thou didst Thy pow'r dis - play,
2. For might - y works for Thee pre - pare, And strengthen ev - 'ry heart;
3. All self con-sume, all sin de - stroy! With ear - nest zeal en - due
4. Speak, Lord! be - fore Thy throne we wait, Thy prom-ise we be - lieve,

With cleansing, pur - i - fy - ing flame De-scend on us to - day.
Come, take pos - ses - sion of Thine own, And nev - er - more de - part.
Each wait - ing heart to wait for Thee; O Lord, our faith re - new!
And will not let Thee go un - til The bless - ing we re - ceive.

Chorus

Lord, send the old-time pow'r, The Pen-te-cost - al pow'r! Thy floodgates of

bless-ing on us throw o - pen wide! Lord, send the old - time pow'r, the

Pen-te-cost - al pow'r, That sinners be converted and Thy name glo-ri-fied!

42 Jesus Loves Even Me

P. P. B.

P. P. BLISS

1. I am so glad that our Fa - ther in heav'n Tells of His
love in the Book He has giv'n, Won - der - ful things in the
Bi - ble I see; This is the dear - est, that Je - sus loves me.

2. Tho' I for - get Him and wan - der a - way, Still He doth
love me wher - ev - er I stray; Back to His dear lov - ing
arms would I flee, When I re - mem - ber that Je - sus loves me.

3. Oh, if there's on - ly one song I can sing, When in His
beau - ty I see the great King, This shall my song in e-
ter - ni - ty be: "Oh, what a won - der that Je - sus loves me."

CHORUS

I am so glad that Je - sus loves me, Je - sus loves me, Je - sus loves me,
I am so glad that Je - sus loves me, Je - sus loves e - ven me.

43 There Shall Be Showers of Blessing

El Nathan

James McGranahan

1. "There shall be show-ers of bless-ing:" This is the prom-ise of love;
2. "There shall be show-ers of bless-ing"—Pre-cious re-viv-ing a-gain;
3. "There shall be show-ers of bless-ing:" Send them up-on us, O Lord;
4. "There shall be show-ers of bless-ing:" Oh, that to-day they might fall,

There shall be sea-sons re-fresh-ing, Sent from the Sav-ior a-bove.
O-ver the hills and the val-leys, Sound of a-bun-dance of rain.
Grant to us now a re-fresh-ing, Come, and now hon-or Thy Word.
Now as to God we're con-fess-ing, Now as on Je-sus we call!

Chorus

Show - - ers of bless-ing, Show-ers of bless-ing we need:
Show - ers, show-ers of bless-ing,

Mer-cy-drops round us are fall-ing, But for the show-ers we plead.

44 Oh! Say, But I'm Glad

Dedicated to Bishop Arthur J. Moore

REV. JAS. P. SULLIVAN

MILDRED ELLEN SULLIVAN

1. There is a song in my heart to-day, Something I nev-er had;
2. Won-der-ful, mar-vel-ous love He brings, In - to a heart that's sad;
3. We have a fel-low-ship rich and sweet, Tongue can nev-er re - late;
4. Won't you come to Him with all your care, Wea-ry and worn and sad?

Je-sus has tak-en my sins a-way, Oh! say, but I'm glad.
Thro' darkest tun-nels the soul just sings, Oh! say, but I'm glad.
Abid-ing in Him is a re - al treat, Oh! say, but it's great.
You too, will sing as His love you share, Oh! say, but I'm glad.

CHORUS

Oh! say, but I'm glad, I'm glad, Oh! say, but I'm glad; (Inst.)

Je-sus has come and my cup's o - ver run, Oh! say, but I'm glad.

45 It Is Well With My Soul

H. G. SPAFFORD

P. P. BLISS

1. When peace, like a riv-er, at-tend-eth my way, When sor-rows like
2. Though Sa-tan should buf-fet, tho' tri-als should come, Let this blest as-
3. My sin— oh, the bliss of this glo-ri-ous tho't—My sin—not in
4. And, Lord, haste the day when the faith shall be sight, The clouds be rolled

sea-bil-lows roll; What-ev-er my lot, Thou hast taught me to say,
sur-ance con-trol, That Christ has re-gard-ed my help-less es-tate,
part, but the whole, Is nailed to the cross and I bear it no more,
back as a scroll, The trump shall re-sound and the Lord shall de-scend,

CHORUS

It is well, it is well with my soul.
And hath shed His own blood for my soul. It is well..... with my
Praise the Lord, praise the Lord, O my soul!
"E-ven so"—it is well with my soul. It is well

soul,...... It is well, it is well with my soul.
with my soul,

46 Are Ye Able, Said the Master

Earl Marlatt

Harry S. Mason

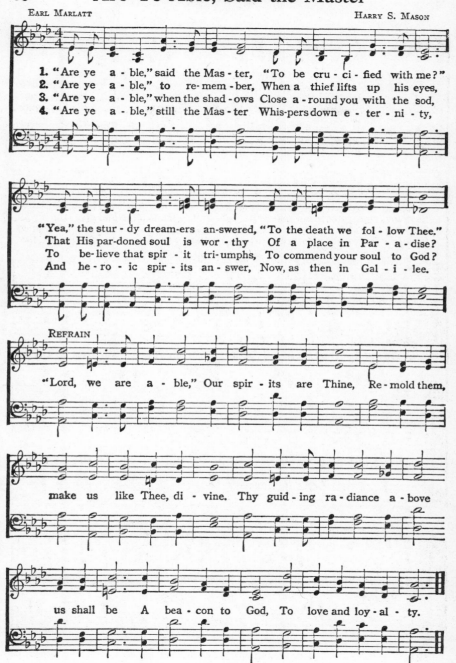

1. "Are ye a - ble," said the Mas - ter, "To be cru - ci - fied with me?"
2. "Are ye a - ble," to re - mem - ber, When a thief lifts up his eyes,
3. "Are ye a - ble," when the shad - ows Close a - round you with the sod,
4. "Are ye a - ble," still the Mas - ter Whis - pers down e - ter - ni - ty,

"Yea," the stur - dy dream - ers an - swered, "To the death we fol - low Thee."
That His par - doned soul is wor - thy Of a place in Par - a - dise?
To be - lieve that spir - it tri - umphs, To commend your soul to God?
And he - ro - ic spir - its an - swer, Now, as then in Gal - i - lee.

REFRAIN

"Lord, we are a - ble," Our spir - its are Thine, Re - mold them, make us like Thee, di - vine. Thy guid - ing ra - diance a - bove us shall be A bea - con to God, To love and loy - al - ty.

47 Living for Jesus

T. O. Chisholm
Not fast

C. Harold Lowden

1. Liv-ing for Je-sus a life that is true, Striving to please Him in all that I do,
2. Liv-ing for Je-sus who died in my place, Bearing on Calv'ry my sin and disgrace,
3. Liv-ing for Je-sus wher-ev-er I am, Do-ing each du-ty in His Ho-ly Name,
4. Living for Jesus thro' earth's little while, My dearest treasure, the light of His smile,

Yielding allegiance, glad-hearted and free, This is the pathway of blessing for me.
Such love constrains me to answer His call, Follow His leading and give Him my all.
Will-ing to suf-fer af-flic-tion or loss, Deeming each trial a part of my cross.
Seek-ing the lost ones He died to redeem, Bringing the weary to find rest in Him.

* CHORUS. UNISON. *A little slower.*

O Je-sus, Lord and Savior, I give my-self to Thee; For Thou, in Thy a-

tonement, Didst give Thyself for me; I own no oth-er Mas-ter, My

rit.............

heart shall be Thy throne, My life I give, henceforth to live. O Christ, for Thee alone.

*Melody in lower notes. A two-part effect may be had by having the men sing the melody, the women taking the middle notes.

48 Since Jesus Came Into My Heart

R. H. McDaniel

Chas. H. Gabriel

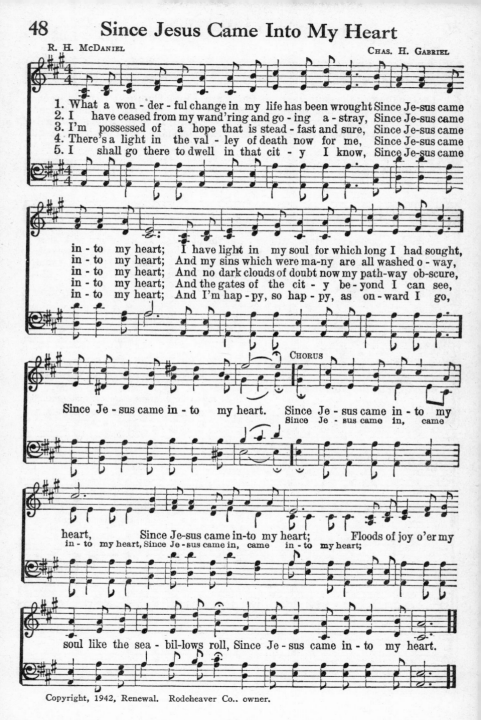

1. What a won-der-ful change in my life has been wrought Since Je-sus came
2. I have ceased from my wand'ring and go-ing a-stray, Since Je-sus came
3. I'm possessed of a hope that is stead-fast and sure, Since Je-sus came
4. There's a light in the val-ley of death now for me, Since Je-sus came
5. I shall go there to dwell in that cit-y I know, Since Je-sus came

in-to my heart; I have light in my soul for which long I had sought,
in-to my heart; And my sins which were ma-ny are all washed o-way,
in-to my heart; And no dark clouds of doubt now my path-way ob-scure,
in-to my heart; And the gates of the cit-y be-yond I can see,
in-to my heart; And I'm hap-py, so hap-py, as on-ward I go,

CHORUS

Since Je-sus came in-to my heart. Since Je-sus came in-to my
Since Je-sus came in, came

heart, Since Je-sus came in-to my heart; Floods of joy o'er my
in-to my heart, Since Je-sus came in, came in-to my heart;

soul like the sea-bil-lows roll, Since Je-sus came in-to my heart.

49 Standing On the Promises

R. K. C. R. Kelso Carter

1. Stand-ing on the prom-is-es of Christ my King, Thro' e-ter-nal a-ges
2. Stand-ing on the prom-is-es that can-not fail, When the howling storms of
3. Stand-ing on the prom-is-es of Christ the Lord, Bound to Him e-ter-nal-
4. Stand-ing on the prom-is-es I can-not fall, Lis-t'ning ev-'ry mo-ment

let His prais-es ring; Glo-ry in the high-est, I will shout and sing,
doubt and fear as-sail, By the liv-ing word of God I shall pre-vail,
ly by love's strong cord, O-ver-com-ing dai-ly with the Spir-it's sword,
to the Spir-it's call, Rest-ing in my Sav-ior, as my all in all,

CHORUS

Stand-ing on the prom-is-es of God. Stand - - ing, stand - - ing,
Standing on the promises, standing on the promises,

Stand-ing on the prom-is-es of God my Sav-ior; Stand - - ing,
Stand-ing on the prom-is-es,

stand - - ing, I'm stand-ing on the prom-is-es of God.
stand-ing on the prom-is-es,

50 Some Bright Morning

CHARLOTTE G. HOMER

CHAS. H. GABRIEL

1. Be not a-wea-ry, for la-bor will cease Some glad morn-ing;
2. Wea-ri-some bur-dens will all be laid down, Some glad morn-ing;
3. La-bor well done shall re-ceive its re-ward, Some glad morn-ing;
4. O what a time of re-joic-ing will come, Some glad morn-ing;
5. There with the loved ones who've gone on be-fore, Some glad morn-ing;

Tur-moil will change in-to in-fi-nite peace, Some bright morn-ing.
Then shall our cross be exchanged for a crown, Some bright morn-ing.
Thou who art faith-ful shall be with the Lord, Some bright morn-ing.
When all the ransomed are gathered at home, Some bright morn-ing.
We shall sing praise to the Lamb ev-er-more, Some bright morn-ing.

CHORUS

Some bright morning, Some glad morn-ing, When the sun is shin-ing

in th' e-ter-nal sky;.... Some bright morn-ing, Some glad

cres.

morn-ing.. We shall see the Lord of Har-vest, By and by.

51 Trust and Obey

J. H. SAMMIS

D. B. TOWNER

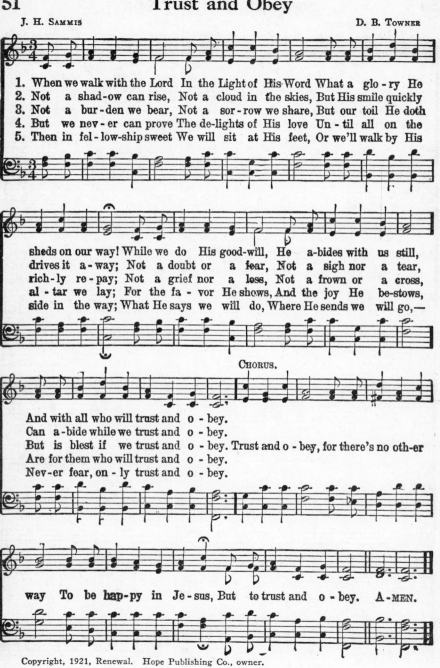

1. When we walk with the Lord In the Light of His Word What a glo-ry He
2. Not a shad-ow can rise, Not a cloud in the skies, But His smile quickly
3. Not a bur-den we bear, Not a sor-row we share, But our toil He doth
4. But we nev-er can prove The de-lights of His love Un-til all on the
5. Then in fel-low-ship sweet We will sit at His feet, Or we'll walk by His

sheds on our way! While we do His good-will, He a-bides with us still,
drives it a-way; Not a doubt or a fear, Not a sigh nor a tear,
rich-ly re-pay; Not a grief nor a loss, Not a frown or a cross,
al-tar we lay; For the fa-vor He shows, And the joy He be-stows,
side in the way; What He says we will do, Where He sends we will go,—

CHORUS.

And with all who will trust and o-bey.
Can a-bide while we trust and o-bey.
But is blest if we trust and o-bey. Trust and o-bey, for there's no oth-er
Are for them who will trust and o-bey.
Nev-er fear, on-ly trust and o-bey.

way To be hap-py in Je-sus, But to trust and o-bey. A-MEN.

52 Open My Eyes That I May See

C. H. S.

CHAS. H. SCOTT

1. O-pen my eyes, that I may see, Glimpses of truth Thou hast for me;
2. O-pen my ears, that I may hear, Voi-ces of truth Thou send-est clear;
3. O-pen my mouth and let me bear Glad-ly the warm truth ev-'ry-where;

Place in my hands the won-der-ful key That shall unclasp, and set me free.
And while the wave-notes fall on my ear, Ev-'ry-thing false will dis-ap-pear.
O-pen my heart and let me prepare Love with Thy chil-dren thus to share.

Si-lent-ly now I wait for Thee, Read-y, my God, Thy will to see;
Si-lent-ly now I wait for Thee, Read-y, my God, Thy will to see;
Si-lent-ly now I wait for Thee, Read-y, my God, Thy will to see;

O-pen my eyes, il-lu-mine me, Spir-it di-vine!
O-pen my ears, il-lu-mine me, Spir-it di-vine!
O-pen my heart, il-lu-mine me, Spir-it di-vine! A-men.

53

Just As I Am

CHARLOTTE ELLIOTT

WILLIAM B. BRADBURY

1. Just as I am, with-out one plea, But that Thy blood was shed for me,
2. Just as I am, and waiting not To rid my soul of one dark blot,
3. Just as I am, tho' tossed a-bout With many a con-flict, many a doubt,
4. Just as I am, poor, wretched, blind; Sight, rich-es, heal-ing of the mind,
5. Just as I am—Thou wilt re-ceive, Wilt welcome, pardon, cleanse, relieve;

And that Thou bidd'st me come to Thee, O Lamb of God, I come! I come!
To Thee whose blood can cleanse each spot, O Lamb of God, I come! I come!
Fight-ings and fears with-in, with-out, O Lamb of God, I come! I come!
Yea, all I need in Thee to find, O Lamb of God, I come! I come!
Be-cause Thy promise I be-lieve, O Lamb of God, I come! I come!

54

Only Trust Him

J. H. S.

J. H. STOCKTON

1. Come, ev-'ry soul by sin oppressed, There's mer-cy with the Lord,
2. For Je-sus shed His pre-cious blood, Rich bless-ings to be-stow;
3. Yes, Je-sus is the Truth, the Way, That leads you in-to rest:
4. Come, then, and join this ho-ly band, And on to glo-ry go,

And He will sure-ly give you rest By trust-ing in His word.
Plunge now in-to the crim-son flood That wash-es white as snow.
Be-lieve in Him with-out de-lay, And you are ful-ly blest.
To dwell in that ce-les-tial land, Where joys im-mor-tal flow.

Only Trust Him

CHORUS

On - ly trust Him, on - ly trust Him, On - ly trust Him now;
He will save you, He will save you, He will (*Omit* . . . .) save you now.

55   Leaning On the Everlasting Arms

E. A. HOFFMAN   A. J. SHOWALTER

1. What a fel-low-ship, what a joy di-vine, Leaning on the ev-er-last-ing arms;
2. Oh, how sweet to walk in this pilgrim way, Leaning on the ev-er-last-ing arms;
3. What have I to dread, what have I to fear, Leaning on the ev-er-last-ing arms?

What a bless-ed-ness, what a peace is mine, Leaning on the ev-er-last-ing arms.
Oh, how bright the path grows from day to day, Leaning on the ev-er-last-ing arms.
I have bless-ed peace with my Lord so near, Leaning on the ev-er-last-ing arms.

REFRAIN

Lean - ing, lean - ing, Safe and se-cure from all a-larms;
Lean-ing on Je - sus, lean-ing on Je - sus,

Lean - ing, lean - ing, Lean-ing on the ev- er-last-ing arms.
Lean-ing on Je - sus, lean-ing on Je - sus,

56 He's a Wonderful Savior to Me

Virgil P. Brock

Blanche Kerr Brock

1. I was lost in sin but Jesus rescued me, He's a wonderful Savior to
2. He's a Friend so true, so patient and so kind, He's a wonderful Savior to
3. He is always near to comfort and to cheer, He's a wonderful Savior to
4. Dearer grows the love of Jesus day by day, He's a wonderful Savior to

me;
me;
me;
me;
So wonderful!

I was bound by fear but Jesus set me free, He's a
Ev'rything I need in Him I always find, He's a
He forgives my sins, He dries my ev'ry tear, He's a
Sweeter is His grace while pressing on my way, He's a

wonderful Savior to me.......... So wonderful!

CHORUS

For He's a wonderful Savior to me, He's a wonderful Savior to me; won-der-ful!

I was lost in sin, but Jesus took me in, He's a wonderful Savior to me.

57 Jesus, I Come

W. T. Sleeper

Geo. C. Stebbins

1. Out of my bond-age, sor-row and night, Je-sus, I come, Je-sus, I come;
2. Out of my shame-ful fail-ure and loss, Je-sus, I come, Je-sus, I come;
3. Out of un-rest and ar-ro-gant pride, Je-sus, I come, Je-sus, I come;
4. Out of the fear and dread of the tomb, Je-sus, I come, Je-sus, I come;

In-to Thy free-dom, glad-ness and light, Je-sus, I come to Thee;
In-to the glo-rious gain of Thy cross, Je-sus, I come to Thee;
In-to Thy bless-ed will to a-bide, Je-sus, I come to Thee;
In-to the joy and light of Thy home, Je-sus, I come to Thee;

Out of my sick-ness in-to Thy health, Out of my want and in-to Thy wealth,
Out of earth's sorrows in-to Thy balm, Out of life's storms and in-to Thy calm,
Out of my-self to dwell in Thy love, Out of de-spair in-to rap-tures a-bove,
Out of the depths of ru-in un-told, In-to the peace of Thy sheltering fold,

Out of my sin and in-to Thy-self, Je-sus, I come to Thee.
Out of dis-tress to ju-bi-lant psalm, Je-sus, I come to Thee.
Up-ward for aye on wings like a dove, Je-sus, I come to Thee.
Ev-er Thy glo-rious face to be-hold, Je-sus, I come to Thee.

58 Jesus Took My Burden

Rev. Johnson Oatman, Jr.

Bertha Mae Lillenas

1. When I, a poor, lost sin-ner, Be-fore the Lord did fall, And in the name of
2. Oft-times the way is drear-y, And rugged seems the road, Oft-times I'm weak and
3. When I was crushed with sorrow I bowed in deep de-spair, My load of grief and
4. I'll trust Him for the fu-ture, He know-eth all the way, For with His eye He'll

Je - sus For par-don loud did call; He heard my sup-pli-ca-tion, And
wea - ry, When bent beneath some load; But when I cry in weak-ness, "How
heart-ache Seemed more than I could bear; 'Twas then I heard a whis-per, "You
guide me A - long life's pil-grim way; And I will tell in heav-en, While

soon the weak was strong, For Je - sus took my bur-den, And left me with a song.
long, O Lord, how long?" Then Je-sus takes the bur-den, And leaves me with a song.
to the Lord be - long," Then Je-sus took my bur-den, And left me with a song.
a - ges roll a - long, How Je-sus took my bur-den, And left me with a song.

CHORUS

Yes, Je-sus took my bur-den I could no lon-ger bear, Yes, Je-sus took my

bur-den In an - swer to my prayer; My anx-ious fears sub-sid-ed, My

Jesus Took My Burden

spir-it was made strong, For Je-sus took my bur-den, And left me with a song.

59 Nothing But the Blood

R. L.

ROBERT LOWRY

1. What can wash a - way my sin? Noth-ing but the blood of Je - sus;
2. For my par - don this I see— Noth-ing but the blood of Je - sus;
3. Noth - ing can for sin a - tone— Noth-ing but the blood of Je - sus;
4. This is all my hope and peace—Noth-ing but the blood of Je - sus;

What can make me whole a - gain? Noth-ing but the blood of Je - sus.
For my cleans-ing, this my plea—Noth-ing but the blood of Je - sus.
Naught of good that I have done—Noth-ing but the blood of Je - sus.
This is all my right-eous - ness—Noth-ing but the blood of Je - sus.

REFRAIN

Oh! pre - cious is the flow That makes me white as snow;

No oth - er fount I know, Noth-ing but the blood of Je - sus.

60 Help Somebody To-day

Mrs. Frank A. Breck

Chas. H. Gabriel

1. Look all a-round you, find some one in need, Help some-bod-y to - day!
2. Man - y are wait-ing a kind, lov-ing word, Help some-bod-y to - day!
3. Man - y have bur-dens too heav - y to bear, Help some-bod-y to - day!
4. Some are dis-cour-aged and wear-y in heart, Help some-bod-y to - day!

Tho' it be lit - tle—a neigh-bor - ly deed—Help some-bod - y to - day!
Thou hast a mes-sage, O let it be heard, Help some-bod - y to - day!
Grief is the por - tion of some ev - 'ry-where, Help some-bod - y to - day!
Some one the jour-ney to Heaven should start, Help some-bod - y to - day!

CHORUS.

Help some-bod - y to - day, . . Some-bod - y a - long life's way; . . Let
to-day,   home-ward way;

sorrow be ended, The friendless befriended, Oh, help somebody to-day! A - MEN.

61 I Will Sing the Wondrous Story

F. H. Rowley

Peter P. Bilhorn

1. I will sing the won-drous sto - ry Of the Christ who died for me,
2. I was lost, but Je - sus found me, Found the sheep that went a - stray,
3. I was bruised, but Je - sus healed me; Faint was I from man-y a fall;
4. Days of dark-ness still come o'er me, Sor-row's paths I oft - en tread.
5. He will keep me till the riv - er Rolls its wa - ters at my feet;

How He left His home in glo - ry For the cross of Cal - va - ry.
Threw His lov - ing arms a - round me, Drew me back in - to His way.
Sight was gone, and fears pos-sessed me, But He freed me from them all.
But the Sav - iour still is with me; By His hand I'm safe - ly led.
Then He'll bear me safe - ly o - ver, Where the loved ones I shall meet.

CHORUS

Yes, I'll sing .... the won-drous sto - ry Of the
Yes, I'll sing   the won-drous sto - ry

Christ .... who died for me, ... Sing it with .... the saints in
Of the Christ   who died for me,   Sing it with

glo - ry, Gath-ered by ...... the crys-tal sea ......
the saints in glo - ry,   Gath-ered by   the crystal sea.

62 Pass Me Not

FANNY J. CROSBY

W. H. DOANE

1. Pass me not, O gen-tle Sav-ior, Hear my hum-ble cry; While on oth-ers
2. Let me at a throne of mer-cy Find a sweet re-lief; Kneel-ing there in
3. Trust-ing on-ly in Thy mer-it, Would I seek Thy face; Heal my wounded,
4. Thou the Spring of all my com-fort, More than life to me, Whom have I on

CHORUS

Thou art call-ing, Do not pass me by.
deep con-tri-tion, Help my un-be-lief. Sav-ior, Sav-ior, Hear my humble
bro-ken spir-it, Save me by Thy grace.
earth beside Thee? Whom in Heav'n but Thee?

cry; While on oth-ers Thou art call-ing, Do not pass me by.

63 Let the Lower Lights Be Burning

P. P. B.

P. P. BLISS

1. Bright-ly beams our Fa-ther's mer-cy From His light-house ev-er-more,
2. Dark the night of sin has set-tled, Loud the an-gry bil-lows roar;
3. Trim your fee-ble lamp, my broth-er: Some poor sail-or tem-pest-tossed,

FINE

But to us He gives the keep-ing Of the lights a-long the shore.
Ea-ger eyes are watching, long-ing, For the lights a-long the shore.
Try-ing now to make the har-bor, In the dark-ness may be lost.

D.S.—*Some poor faint-ing, struggling sea-man You may res-cue, you may save.*

Let the Lower Lights Be Burning

D.S.

Let the low-er lights be burn-ing! Send a gleam a-cross the wave!

64 Shall We Gather at the River?

R. L.
ROBERT LOWRY

1. Shall we gath-er at the riv-er, Where bright an-gel feet have trod;
2. On the bos-om of the riv-er, Where the Sav-ior-King we own,
3. Ere we reach the shin-ing riv-er, Lay we ev-'ry bur-den down;
4. Soon we'll reach the shining riv-er, Soon our pil-grim-age will cease;

With its crys-tal tide for-ev-er Flow-ing by the throne of God?
We shall meet, and sor-row nev-er, 'Neath the glo-ry of the throne.
Grace our spir-its will de-liv-er, And pro-vide a robe and crown.
Soon our hap-py hearts will qui-ver With the mel-o-dy of peace.

CHORUS

Yes, we'll gather at the riv-er, The beau-ti-ful, the beau-ti-ful riv-er,

Gath-er with the saints at the riv-er That flows by the throne of God.

65 The Beautiful Garden of Prayer

ELEANOR ALLEN SCHROLL

J. H. FILLMORE

1. There's a gar-den where Je-sus is wait-ing, There's a place that is
2. There's a gar-den where Je-sus is wait-ing, And I go with my
3. There's a gar-den where Je-sus is wait-ing, And He bids you to

won-drous-ly fair; For it glows with the light of His pres-ence, 'Tis the
bur-den and care, Just to learn from His lips words of com-fort, In the
come meet Him there; Just to bow and re-ceive a new bless-ing, In the

beau-ti-ful gar-den of pray'r.

REFRAIN

O the beau-ti-ful gar-den, the

garden of pray'r, O the beau-ti-ful gar-den of pray'r; There my Savior a-

waits, and He o-pens the gates To the beau-ti-ful gar-den of pray'r.

66 Does Jesus Care?

Frank E. Graeff

J. Lincoln Hall

1. Does Je-sus care when my heart is pained Too deep-ly for
2. Does Je-sus care when my way is dark With a name-less
3. Does Je-sus care when I've tried and failed To re-sist some temp-
4. Does Je-sus care when I've said "good-bye" To the dear-est on

mirth or song, As the bur-dens press, And the cares dis-tress,
dread and fear? As the day-light fades In-to deep night shades,
ta-tion strong; When for my deep grief There is no re-lief,
earth to me, And my sad heart aches Till it near-ly breaks,

Refrain

And the way grows wea-ry and long?
Does He care e-nough to be near? O yes, He cares, I
Tho' my tears flow all the night long?
Is it aught to Him? does He see?

know He cares, His heart is touched with my grief; . . When the days are

wea-ry, The long night drear-y, I know my Sav-iour cares. . .
He cares.

67 Let Him In

E. O. Excell

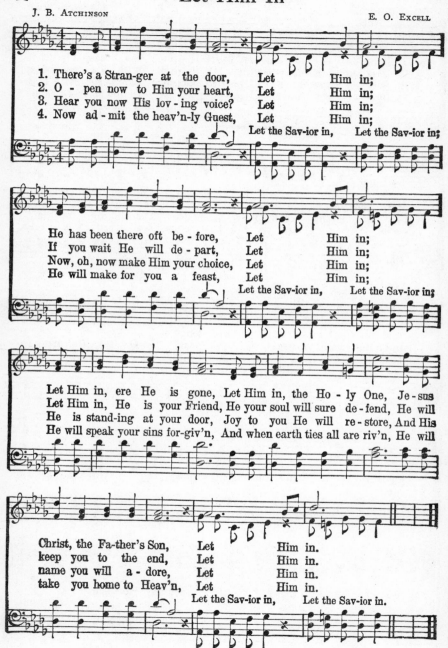

1. There's a Stran-ger at the door, Let Him in;
2. O - pen now to Him your heart, Let Him in;
3. Hear you now His lov - ing voice? Let Him in;
4. Now ad - mit the heav'n-ly Guest, Let Him in;

Let the Sav-ior in, Let the Sav-ior in;

He has been there oft be - fore, Let Him in;
If you wait He will de - part, Let Him in;
Now, oh, now make Him your choice, Let Him in;
He will make for you a feast, Let Him in;

Let the Sav-ior in, Let the Sav-ior in;

Let Him in, ere He is gone, Let Him in, the Ho - ly One, Je-sus
Let Him in, He is your Friend, He your soul will sure de - fend, He will
He is stand-ing at your door, Joy to you He will re - store, And His
He will speak your sins for-giv'n, And when earth ties all are riv'n, He will

Christ, the Fa-ther's Son, Let Him in.
keep you to the end, Let Him in.
name you will a - dore, Let Him in.
take you home to Heav'n, Let Him in.

Let the Sav-ior in, Let the Sav-ior in.

68 The Gospel According to You

W. C. POOLE

GEORGE W. COOKE

1. A Gos-pel was writ-ten by Mat-thew of old, A rec-ord so
2. Four Gos-pels were writ-ten of Je-sus, your Lord, That oth-ers His
3. Your serv-ice, de-vo-tion, your life and your love, For Je-sus and

faith-ful and true; But man-y are read-ing the life you un-fold—
good-ness might view; But man-y are read-ing who miss His true Word—
oth-ers so true, Are read here at home and in heav-en a-bove—

CHORUS

The Gos-pel ac-cord-ing to you. . . . . . The Gos-pel ac-cord-ing to
ac-cord-ing to you. The Gos-pel ac-

you, ... Of all that you say and you do; . , ... Wher-
cord-ing to you, Of all that you say and you do;

ev-er you go, let your life tru-ly show The Gos-pel ac-cord-ing to you.

69   I Am Coming Home

A. H. ACKLEY

B. D. ACKLEY

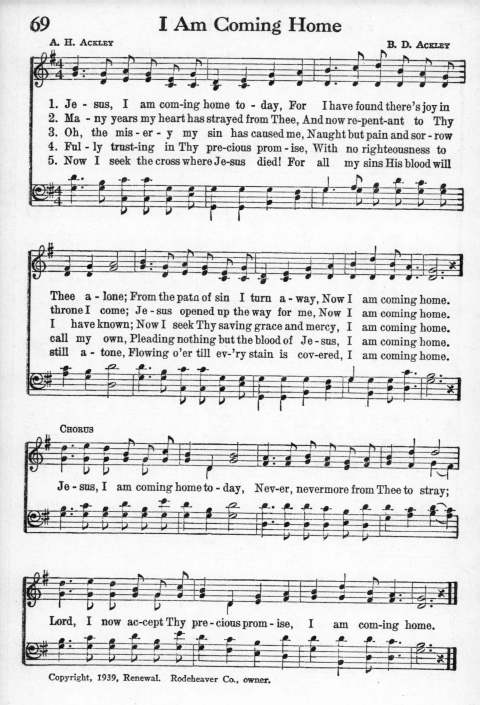

1. Je - sus, I am com-ing home to - day, For I have found there's joy in
2. Ma - ny years my heart has strayed from Thee, And now re-pent-ant to Thy
3. Oh, the mis - er - y my sin has caused me, Naught but pain and sor - row
4. Ful - ly trust-ing in Thy pre-cious prom - ise, With no righteousness to
5. Now I seek the cross where Je-sus died! For all my sins His blood will

Thee a - lone; From the path of sin I turn a - way, Now I am coming home.
throne I come; Je - sus opened up the way for me, Now I am coming home.
I have known; Now I seek Thy saving grace and mercy, I am coming home.
call my own, Pleading nothing but the blood of Je - sus, I am coming home.
still a - tone, Flowing o'er till ev-'ry stain is cov-ered, I am coming home.

CHORUS

Je - sus, I am coming home to - day, Nev-er, nevermore from Thee to stray;

Lord, I now ac-cept Thy pre - cious prom - ise, I am com-ing home.

The Haven of Rest

H. L. GILMOUR

GEORGE D. MOORE

1. My soul in sad ex-ile was out on life's sea, So burdened with
2. I yield-ed my-self to His ten-der em-brace, And faith tak-ing
3. The song of my soul, since the Lord made me whole, Has been the old
4. How pre-cious the tho't that we all may re-cline, Like John the be-
5. O come to the Sav-ior, He pa-tient-ly waits To save by His

sin and dis-tressed, Till I heard a sweet voice saying, "Make me your choice;"
hold of the Word, My fet-ters fell off, and I an-chored my soul;
sto-ry so blest, Of Je-sus who'll save who-so-ev-er will have
lov-ed and blest, On Je-sus' strong arm, where no tem-pest can harm,
pow-er di-vine; Come, an-chor your soul in the "Ha-ven of Rest,"

CHORUS

And I entered the "Ha-ven of Rest."
The "Ha-ven of Rest" is my Lord.
A home in the "Ha-ven of Rest." I've anchored my soul in the
Se-cure in the "Ha-ven of Rest."
And say, "My Be-lov-ed is mine."

"Ha-ven of Rest," I'll sail the wide seas no more; The tempest may

sweep o'er the wild storm-y deep; In Je-sus I'm safe ev-er-more.

71 The Unclouded Day

J. K. A.

Rev. J. K. Alwood

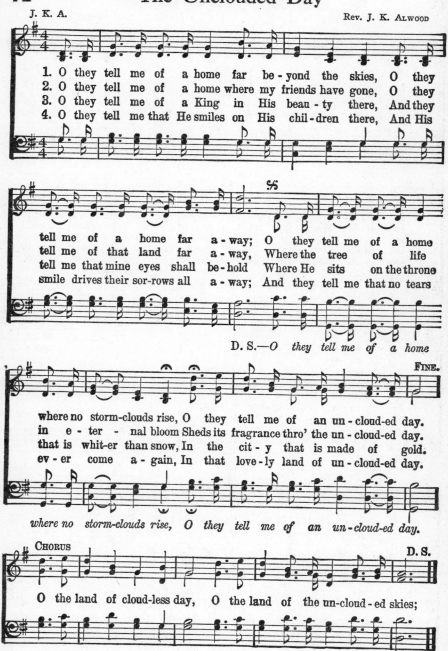

1. O they tell me of a home far be-yond the skies, O they
2. O they tell me of a home where my friends have gone, O they
3. O they tell me of a King in His beau-ty there, And they
4. O they tell me that He smiles on His chil-dren there, And His

tell me of a home far a-way; O they tell me of a home
tell me of that land far a-way, Where the tree of life
tell me that mine eyes shall be-hold Where He sits on the throne
smile drives their sor-rows all a-way; And they tell me that no tears

D. S.—*O they tell me of a home*

where no storm-clouds rise, O they tell me of an un-cloud-ed day.
in e-ter-nal bloom Sheds its fragrance thro' the un-cloud-ed day.
that is whit-er than snow, In the cit-y that is made of gold.
ev-er come a-gain, In that love-ly land of un-cloud-ed day.

FINE.

where no storm-clouds rise, O they tell me of an un-cloud-ed day.

CHORUS

D. S.

O the land of cloud-less day, O the land of the un-cloud-ed skies;

72 For You I Am Praying

S. O'MALEY CLUFF

IRA D. SANKEY

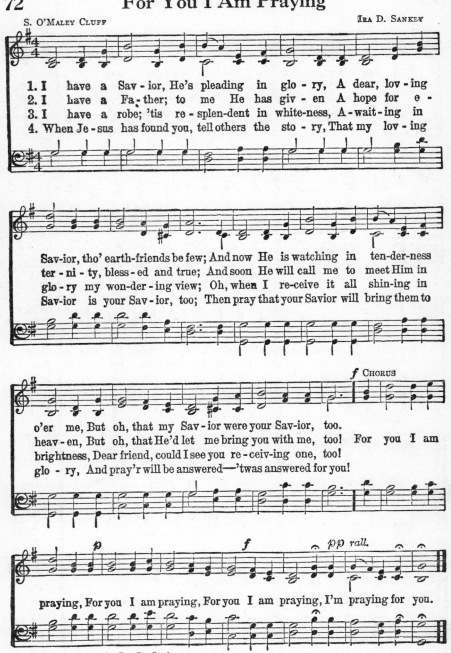

1. I have a Sav-ior, He's pleading in glo-ry, A dear, lov-ing
2. I have a Fa-ther; to me He has giv-en A hope for e-
3. I have a robe; 'tis re-splen-dent in white-ness, A-wait-ing in
4. When Je-sus has found you, tell others the sto-ry, That my lov-ing

Sav-ior, tho' earth-friends be few; And now He is watching in ten-der-ness
ter-ni-ty, bless-ed and true; And soon He will call me to meet Him in
glo-ry my won-der-ing view; Oh, when I re-ceive it all shin-ing in
Sav-ior is your Sav-ior, too; Then pray that your Savior will bring them to

o'er me, But oh, that my Sav-ior were your Sav-ior, too.
heav-en, But oh, that He'd let me bring you with me, too! For you I am
brightness, Dear friend, could I see you re-ceiv-ing one, too!
glo-ry, And pray'r will be answered—'twas answered for you!

f CHORUS

praying, For you I am praying, For you I am praying, I'm praying for you.

73 Love Lifted Me

JAMES ROWE

HOWARD E. SMITH

1. I was sink-ing deep in sin, Far from the peaceful shore, Ver-y deep-ly
2. All my heart to Him I give, Ev-er to Him I'll cling, In His bless-ed
3. Souls in dan-ger, look a-bove, Je-sus com-plete-ly saves; He will lift you

stained with-in, Sink-ing to rise no more; But the Mas-ter of the sea
pres-ence live, Ev-er His prais-es sing. Love so might-y and so true
by His love Out of the an-gry waves. He's the Mas-ter of the sea,

Heard my despairing cry, From the wa-ters lift-ed me, Now safe am I.
Mer-its my soul's best songs; Faith-ful, lov-ing serv-ice, too, To Him be-longs.
Bil-lows His will o-bey; He your Sav-ior wants to be—Be saved to-day.

CHORUS

Love lift-ed me!.... Love lift-ed me!.... When noth-ing
e - ven me!   e - ven me!

1. else could help, Love lift-ed me.
2. Love lift-ed me.

74 Jesus Will!

INA DULEY OGDON

B. D. ACKLEY

1. Who will o-pen mer-cy's door? Je-sus will!   Je-sus will!
2. Who can take a-way my sin? Je-sus will!   Je-sus will!
3. Who can conquer doubts and fears? Je-sus will!   Je-sus will!
4. Who will be my dearest Friend? Je-sus will!   Je-sus will!

Je-sus will!   Je-sus will!

As for par-don I im-plore? Je-sus, bless-ed Je-sus will!
Make me pure, with-out, with-in? Je-sus, bless-ed Je-sus will!
Share my joys and dry my tears? Je-sus, bless-ed Je-sus will!
Love and keep me to the end? Je-sus, bless-ed Je-sus will!

REFRAIN.

Je-sus will, Je-sus will! Yes, your lov-ing Sav-ior will;

sure-ly will;

He will each and ev-'ry need ful-fill, Je-sus, bless-ed Je-sus will! A-MEN.

75 Throw Out the Life-Line

Edward S. Ufford

E. S. Ufford
Arr. by George C. Stebbins

1. Throw out the Life-Line a - cross the dark wave, There is a broth - er whom
2. Throw out the Life-Line with hand quick and strong: Why do you tar - ry, why
3. Throw out the Life-Line to dan-ger-fraught men, Sink-ing in an-guish where
4. Soon will the sea - son of res - cue be o'er, Soon will they drift to e -

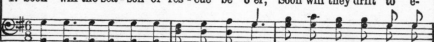

some one should save; Somebody's broth-er! oh, who then, will dare To throw out the
lin - ger so long? See! he is sink-ing; oh; has-ten to-day—And out with the
you've nev-er been: Winds of temp-ta-tion and bil-lows of woe Will soon hurl them
ter - ni-ty's shore, Haste then, my brother, no time for de-lay, But throw out the

Chorus.

Life-Line, his per - il to share?
Life-Boat! a-way, then, a-way! Throw out the Life-Line! Throw out the Life-Line!
out where the dark wa-ters flow.
Life-Line and save them to-day.

Some one is drift-ing a - way; Some one is sink-ing to-day. A - men.

76 The Rock That Is Higher Than I

E. Johnson

William G. Fischer

1. O some-times the shadows are deep, And rough seems the path to the goal,
2. O sometimes how long seems the day, And sometimes how wea-ry my feet;
3. O near to the Rock let me keep, If bless-ings or sor-rows pre-vail;

And sorrows, sometimes how they sweep Like tempests down o-ver the soul!
But toil-ing in life's dust-y way, The Rock's blessed shadow, how sweet!
Or climb-ing the mountain way steep, Or walk-ing the shad-ow-y vale.

REFRAIN

O then to the Rock let me fly, let me fly, To the Rock that is high-er than I; is high-er than I; O then to the Rock let me fly, let me fly, To the Rock that is high-er than I!

77 The Glory of His Presence

REV. OSWALD J. SMITH

B. D. ACKLEY

SOLO

1. I have walked a-lone with Je-sus In a fel-low-ship di-vine;
2. On the moun-tain I have seen Him, Christ my Com-fort-er and Friend;
3. In my fail-ure, sin and sor-row, Bro-ken-heart-ed, crushed and torn,
4. In the dark-ness, in the shad-ow, With the Sav-iour I have trod,

Nev-er-more can earth al-lure me, I am His and He is mine.
And the glo-ry of that vi-sion Will be with me to the end.
I have felt His pres-ence near me, He has all my bur-dens borne.
Sweet in-deed have been the les-sons, Since I've walked a-lone with God.

CHORUS

I have seen Him, I have known Him, For He deigns to walk with me; And the glo-ry of His pres-ence will be mine e-ter-nal-ly. O the glo-ry of His pres-ence, O the beau-ty of His face; I am His and His for-ev-er, He has won me by His grace.

78 The Way of the Cross Leads Home

JESSIE BROWN POUNDS

CHAS. H. GABRIEL

1. I must needs go home by the way of the cross, There's no oth-er
2. I must needs go on in the blood-sprinkled way, The path that the
3. Then I bid fare-well to the way of the world, To walk in it

way but this; I shall ne'er get sight of the Gates of Light,
Sav-ior trod, If I ev-er climb to the heights sub-lime,
nev-er-more; For my Lord says "Come," and I seek my home,

CHORUS.

If the way of the cross I miss.
Where the soul is at home with God. The way of the cross leads
Where He waits at the o-pen door.

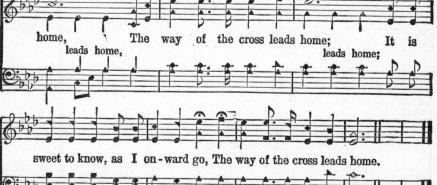

home, The way of the cross leads home; It is
leads home, leads home;

sweet to know, as I on-ward go, The way of the cross leads home.

79 My Savior's Love

C. H. G.

Chas. H. Gabriel

1. I stand a-mazed in the pres-ence Of Je-sus the Naz-a-rene,
2. For me it was in the gar-den He prayed: "Not My will, but Thine;"
3. In pit-y an-gels be-held Him, And came from the world of light
4. He took my sins and my sor-rows, He made them His ver-y own;
5. When with the ransomed in glo-ry His face I at last shall see,

And won-der how He could love me, A sin-ner, condemned, un-clean.
He had no tears for His own griefs, But sweat-drops of blood for mine.
To com-fort Him in the sor-rows He bore for my soul that night.
He bore the bur-den to Cal-v'ry, And suf-fered, and died a-lone.
'Twill be my joy thro' the a-ges To sing of His love for me.

CHORUS.

How mar-vel-ous! how won-der-ful! And my song shall ev-er be:
Oh, how mar-vel-ous! oh, how won-der-ful!

How mar-vel-ous! how won-der-ful Is my Sav-ior's love for me!
Oh, how mar-vel-ous! oh, how won-der-ful

80　In the Service of the King

A. H. ACKLEY

B. D. ACKLEY

1. I am hap-py in the serv-ice of the King, I am hap-py,
2. I am hap-py in the serv-ice of the King, I am hap-py,
3. I am hap-py in the serv-ice of the King, I am hap-py,
4. I am hap-py in the serv-ice of the King, I am hap-py,

oh, so hap-py; I have peace and joy that noth-ing else can bring,
oh, so hap-py; Thru the sun-shine and the shad-ow I can sing,
oh, so hap-py; To His guid-ing hand for-ev-er I will cling,
oh, so hap-py; All that I pos-sess to Him I glad-ly bring,

REFRAIN

In the serv-ice of the King. In the serv-ice of the King Ev-'ry tal-ent I will bring; I have peace and joy and bless-ing In the serv-ice of the King.

81 Christ Receiveth Sinful Men

Arr. from NEUMASTER, 1671

JAMES McGRANAHAN

1. Sin - ners Je - sus will re - ceive; Sound this word of grace to all
2. Come, and He will give you rest; Trust Him, for His word is plain;
3. Now my heart con - demns me not, Pure be - fore the law I stand;
4. Christ re - ceiv - eth sin - ful men, E - ven me with all my sin;

Who the heav'n - ly path-way leave, All who lin - ger, all who fall.
He will take the sin - ful - est; Christ re - ceiv - eth sin - ful men.
He who cleansed me from all spot, Sat - is - fied its last de - mand.
Purged from ev - 'ry spot and stain, Heav'n with Him I en - ter in.

REFRAIN

Sing it o'er...... and o'er a - gain;...... Christ re-
Sing it o'er a-gain, Sing it o'er a-gain; Christ re-

ceiv - - - eth sin-ful men;..... Make the mes - - - sage
ceiv-eth sin - ful men, Christ re-ceiv-eth sin - ful men; Make the message plain,

clear and plain:...... Christ re - ceiv - eth sin - ful men.
Make the mes-sage plain:

82 Sweet By and By

S. F. Bennett   J. P. Webster

1. There's a land that is fair-er than day, And by faith we can
2. We shall sing on that beau-ti-ful shore The mel-o-di-ous
3. To our boun-ti-ful Fa-ther a-bove, We will of-fer our

see it a-far; For the Fa-ther waits o-ver the way, To pre-
songs of the blest, And our spir-its shall sor-row no more, Not a
trib-ute of praise, For the glo-ri-ous gift of His love, And the

Chorus

pare us a dwell-ing-place there. In the sweet by and
sigh for the bless-ing of rest. In the sweet
bless-ings that hal-low our days.

by, by and by, We shall meet on that beau-ti-ful shore; In the

sweet by and by, We shall meet on that beau-ti-ful shore.
In the sweet by and by,

83 Holy Quietness

M. P. FERGUSON

Arr. from W. S. MARSHALL

1. Joys are flow-ing like a riv - er, Since the Com-fort - er has come;
2. Spring-ing in - to life and gladness, All a-round this glorious Guest,
3. Like a rain that falls from heav-en, Like the sun-light from the sky,
4. What a won-der - ful sal - va - tion, Where we al - ways see His face!

He a - bides with us for - ev - er, Makes the trust-ing heart His home.
Ban-ished un - be - lief and sad-ness, And we just o - bey and trust.
So the Ho - ly Ghost is giv - en, Com - ing on us from on high.
What a peaceful hab - i - ta - tion, What a qui - et rest-ing place.

CHORUS

Blessed qui - et-ness, ho - ly qui-et-ness, What as - sur - ance in my soul;

On the storm-y sea, Speaking peace to me, How the bil-lows cease to roll.

84 The Ninety and Nine

Elizabeth C. Clephane

Ira D. Sankey

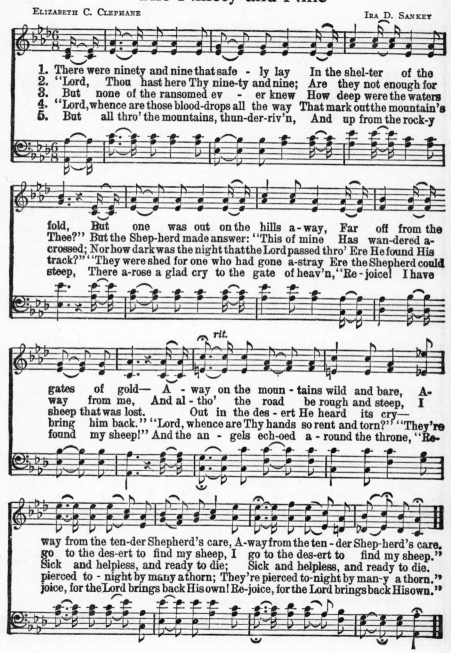

1. There were ninety and nine that safe - ly lay   In the shel-ter of the
2. "Lord,   Thou hast here Thy nine-ty and nine; Are they not enough for
3. But   none of the ransomed ev - er knew How deep were the waters
4. "Lord, whence are those blood-drops all the way That mark out the mountain's
5. But   all thro' the mountains, thun-der-riv'n,   And up from the rock-y

fold, But   one   was out on the hills a-way, Far   off from the
Thee?" But the Shep-herd made answer: "This of mine   Has wan-dered a-
crossed; Nor how dark was the night that the Lord passed thro' Ere He found His
track?" "They were shed for one who had gone a-stray Ere the Shepherd could
steep, There a-rose a glad cry to the gate of heav'n, "Re - joice! I have

rit.

gates   of gold— A - way on the moun - tains wild and bare, A-
way   from me, And al - tho'   the road   be rough and steep,   I
sheep that was lost.   Out in the des - ert He heard   its cry—
bring   him back." "Lord, whence are Thy hands so rent and torn?" "They're
found   my sheep!" And the an - gels ech-oed a - round the throne, "Re-

way from the ten-der Shepherd's care, A-way from the ten - der Shep-herd's care.
go   to the des-ert to find my sheep, I go to the des-ert to   find my sheep."
Sick   and helpless, and ready to die;   Sick and helpless, and ready to die.
pierced to - night by many a thorn; They're pierced to-night by man-y a thorn."
joice, for the Lord brings back His own! Re-joice, for the Lord brings back His own."

85 A Memory

A. H. A.

A. H. ACKLEY

1. With-in my heart I hold a fade-less mem-o-ry, The dear-est
2. He lov-ing-ly for-gave me all my wast-ed years, And filled my
3. No chang-ing scenes of earth can steal my Lord a-way, No veil but

mem-o-ry I know, The mem-o-ry of One who died on
soul with peace di-vine; Such love as I had nev-er known dis-
sin can find His face; He is my ev-er-last-ing strength from

Cal-va-ry, Whose heart was bro-ken by my sin and woe.
pelled my fears, When Je-sus Christ transformed this life of mine.
day to day, And I am kept by His a-bound-ing grace.

CHORUS

Mem-o-ry, mem-o-ry, Bless-ed mem-o-ry that
Sweet mem-o-ry, dear mem-o-ry,

leads me back to Cal-va-ry; When I was lost the Sav-ior found me,

A Memory

Put His lov-ing arms a-round me, 'Tis a mem-o-ry that nev-er fades.

86 I Would Be Like Jesus

JAMES ROWE

B. D. ACKLEY

1. Earth-ly pleas-ures vain-ly call me; I would be like Je - sus;
2. He has bro-ken ev - 'ry fet - ter, I would be like Je - sus;
3. All the way from earth to Glo - ry, I would be like Je - sus;
4. That in heav - en He may meet me, I would be like Je - sus;
would be like Je - sus;

Noth-ing world-ly shall en-thrall me; I would be like Je - sus.
That my soul may serve Him bet - ter, I would be like Je - sus.
Tell - ing o'er and o'er the sto - ry, I would be like Je - sus.
That His words "Well done" may greet me, I would be like Je - sus.
would be like Je - sus.

CHORUS

Be like Je - sus, this my song, In the home and in the throng;

Be like Je - sus, all day long! I would be like Je - sus.

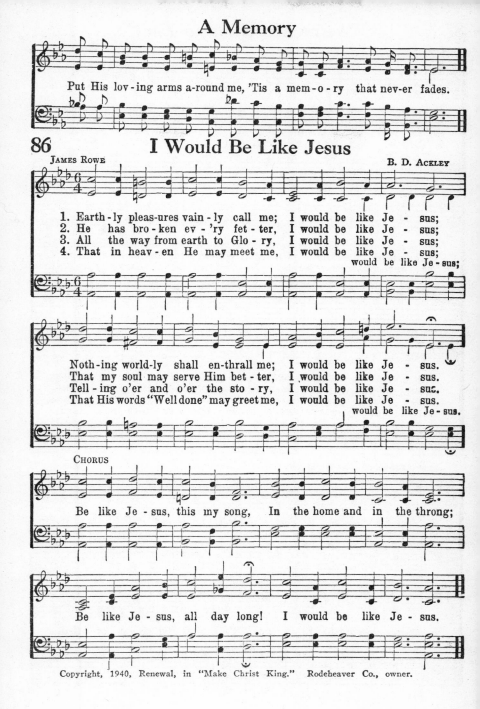

We're Marching to Zion

Isaac Watts
Robert Lowry
Spirited

1. Come, we that love the Lord, And let our joys be known, Join
2. Let those re - fuse to sing Who nev - er knew our God; But
3. The hill of Zi - on yields A thou - sand sa - cred sweets Be-
4. Then let our songs a - bound, And ev - 'ry tear be dry; We're

in a song with sweet ac - cord, Join in a song with sweet ac-cord, And
chil-dren of the heav'n-ly King, But chil-dren of the heav'n-ly King, May
fore we reach the heav'n-ly fields, Be - fore we reach the heav'n-ly fields, Or
marching thro' Immanuel's ground, We're marching thro' Immanuel's ground, To

thus sur - - round the throne, And thus sur-round the throne.
speak their joys a - broad, May speak their joys a - broad.
walk the gold - en streets, Or walk the gold - en streets.
fair - - er worlds on high, To fair - er worlds on high.

thus sur-round the throne, And thus sur - round the throne.

Chorus

We're march - ing to Zi - on, Beau-ti - ful, beau-ti - ful Zi - on; We're
We're march-ing on to Zi - on,

march-ing up-ward to Zi - on, The beau-ti - ful cit - y of God.
Zi - on, Zi - on,

88 O That Will Be Glory

C. H. G.

CHAS. H. GABRIEL

1. When all my la-bors and tri-als are o'er, And I am safe on that
2. When, by the gift of His in-fi-nite grace, I am ac-cord-ed in
3. Friends will be there I have loved long a-go; Joy like a riv-er a-

beau-ti-ful shore, Just to be near the dear Lord I a-dore,
heav-en a place, Just to be there and to look on His face,
round me will flow; Yet, just a smile from my Sav-ior, I know,

rit.

CHORUS. *Faster.*

Will thro' the a-ges be glo-ry for me.... O that will be

glo-ry for me, Glo-ry for me, glo-ry for me; When by His grace
be glo-ry for me, glo-ry for me, glo-ry for me;

rit.

I shall look on His face, That will be glo-ry, be glo-ry for me.

89 I Must Tell Jesus

E. A. H.

E. A. Hoffman

1. I must tell Jesus all of my tri - als; I can - not bear these
2. I must tell Jesus all of my troub - les; He is a kind, com -
3. Tempted and tried I need a great Sav - ior, One who can help my
4. O how the world to e - vil al - lures me! O how my heart is

bur - dens a - lone; In my dis - tress He kind-ly will help me;
pas - sion - ate Friend; If I but ask Him, He will de - liv - er,
bur - dens to bear; I must tell Je - sus, I must tell Je - sus;
tempt - ed to sin! I must tell Je - sus, and He will help me

He ev - er loves and cares for His own.
Make of my troub - les quick - ly an end.
He all my cares and sor - rows will share.
O - ver the world the vic - t'ry to win.

Chorus

I must tell Je - sus!

I must tell Je - sus! I can-not bear my bur - dens a - lone; I must tell

Je - sus! I must tell Je - sus! Je - sus can help me, Je - sus a - lone.

Wonderful Peace

W. D. Cornell. Alt.

W. G. Cooper

1. Far a - way in the depths of my spir - it to - night Rolls a
2. What a treas - ure I have in this won - der - ful peace, Bur - ied
3. I am rest - ing to - night in this won - der - ful peace, Rest - ing
4. And me-thinks when I rise to that Cit - y of peace, Where the
5. Ah! soul, are you here with-out com - fort or rest, March-ing

mel - o - dy sweet-er than psalm; In ce - les - tial-like strains it un-
deep in the heart of my soul; So se - cure that no pow - er can
sweet-ly in Je - sus' con - trol; For I'm kept from all dan - ger by
Au - thor of peace I shall see, That one strain of the song which the
down the rough pathway of time? Make Je - sus your friend ere the

ceas - ing - ly falls O'er my soul like an in - fi - nite calm.
mine it a - way, While the years of e - ter - ni - ty roll.
night and by day, And His glo - ry is flood - ing my soul.
ran - somed will sing, In that heav - en - ly king - dom shall be:
shad - ows grow dark; Oh, ac - cept this sweet peace so sub - lime.

CHORUS

Peace! peace! won-der-ful peace, Com-ing down from the Fa-ther a - bove; Sweep

o - ver my spir - it for - ev - er, I pray, In fath-om-less bil-lows of love.

91 The Old Rugged Cross

Rev. Geo. Bennard

Rev. Geo. Bennard

1. On a hill far a-way stood an old rugged cross, The emblem of
2. Oh, that old rugged cross, so despised by the world, Has a wondrous at -
3. In the old rugged cross, stained with blood so di-vine, A won - drous
4. To the old rugged cross I will ev - er be true, Its shame and re -

suf - f'ring and shame; And I love that old cross where the dear - est and best
trac - tion for me; For the dear Lamb of God left His glo - ry a - bove
beau - ty I see; For 'twas on that old cross Je - sus suf - fered and died
proach glad-ly bear; Then He'll call me some day to my home far a - way,

CHORUS.

For a world of lost sin-ners was slain. So I'll cher-ish the old rug-ged
To bear it to dark Cal - va - ry.
To par - don and sanc-ti - fy me.
Where His glo - ry for - ev - er I'll share.

cross, the

cross, ... Till my tro-phies at last I lay down; I will cling to the
old rug-ged cross,

old rug-ged cross, ... And exchange it some day for a crown.
cross, the old rugged cross,

92 The Lily of the Valley

English Melody

1. I have found a friend in Je-sus, He's ev-'ry-thing to me, He's the fair-est of ten thou-sand to my soul; The Lil-y of the Val-ley, in Him a-lone I see All I need to cleanse and make me ful-ly whole. In sor-row He's my com-fort, in troub-le He's my stay, He tells me ev-'ry care on Him to roll. He's the

2. He all my grief has tak-en, and all my sor-rows borne; In temp-ta-tion He's my strong and mighty tow'r; I have all for Him for-sak-en, and all my i-dols torn From my heart, and now He keeps me by His pow'r. Though all the world for-sake me, and Sa-tan tempts me sore, Through Je-sus I shall safe-ly reach the goal; He's the

3. He will nev-er, nev-er leave me, nor yet for-sake me here, While I live by faith and do His bless-ed will; A wall of fire a-bout me, I've noth-ing now to fear, With His man-na He my hun-gry soul shall fill. Then sweep-ing up to glo-ry, to see His bless-ed face, Where riv-ers of de-light shall ev-er roll! Hal-le-lu-jah! He's the

D. S.—Lil-y of the Val-ley, the bright and Morn-ing Star, He's the fair-est of ten thou-sand to my soul.

FINE

D. S.

93 He Is So Precious to Me

C. H. G.

CHAS. H. GABRIEL

1. So pre-cious is Je-sus, my Sav-ior, my King, His praise all the day
2. He stood at my heart's door 'mid sunshine and rain, And pa-tient-ly wait-
3. I stand on the moun-tain of bless-ing at last, No cloud in the heav-
4. I praise Him be-cause He ap-point-ed a place Where, some day, thro' faith

long with rap-ture I sing; To Him in my weak-ness for strength I can cling,
ed an en-trance to gain; What shame that so long He en-treat-ed in vain,
ens a shad-ow to cast; His smile is up-on me, the val-ley is past,
in His won-der-ful grace, I know I shall see Him—shall look on His face,

CHORUS. *Faster.*

For He is so pre-cious to me. For He is so pre-cious to me, ...
so pre-cious to me,

For He is so pre-cious to me; . . . . 'Tis Heav-en be-low
so pre-cious to me;

rit. . .

My Re-deem-er to know, For He is so pre-cious to me. A-MEN.

94

Jesus Saves

Priscilla J. Owens

Wm. J. Kirkpatrick

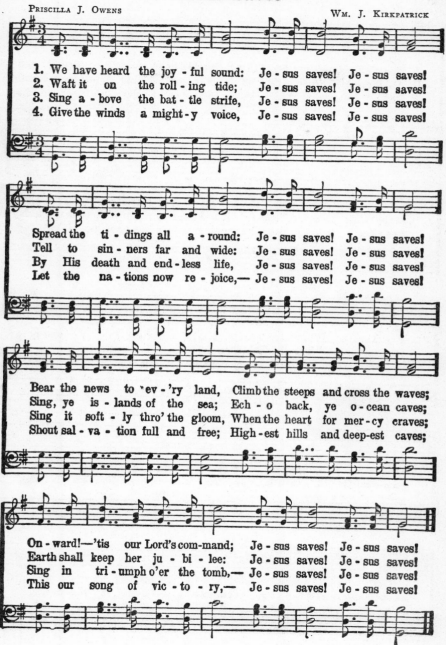

1. We have heard the joy - ful sound: Je - sus saves! Je - sus saves!
2. Waft it on the roll - ing tide; Je - sus saves! Je - sus saves!
3. Sing a - bove the bat - tle strife, Je - sus saves! Je - sus saves!
4. Give the winds a might - y voice, Je - sus saves! Je - sus saves!

Spread the ti - dings all a - round: Je - sus saves! Je - sus saves!
Tell to sin - ners far and wide: Je - sus saves! Je - sus saves!
By His death and end - less life, Je - sus saves! Je - sus saves!
Let the na - tions now re - joice,— Je - sus saves! Je - sus saves!

Bear the news to ev - 'ry land, Climb the steeps and cross the waves;
Sing, ye is - lands of the sea; Ech - o back, ye o - cean caves;
Sing it soft - ly thro' the gloom, When the heart for mer - cy craves;
Shout sal - va - tion full and free; High - est hills and deep - est caves;

On - ward!—'tis our Lord's com - mand; Je - sus saves! Je - sus saves!
Earth shall keep her ju - bi - lee: Je - sus saves! Je - sus saves!
Sing in tri - umph o'er the tomb,— Je - sus saves! Je - sus saves!
This our song of vic - to - ry,— Je - sus saves! Je - sus saves!

95 Constantly Abiding

Mrs. W. L. M.   Mrs. Will L. Murphy

1. There's a peace in my heart that the world nev-er gave, A peace it can
2. All the world seemed to sing of a Sav-ior and King, When peace sweetly
3. This treas-ure I have in a tem-ple of clay, While here on His

not take a - way; Tho' the tri - als of life may sur-round like a cloud,
came to my heart; Troub-les all fled a - way and my night turned to day,
foot-stool I roam; But He's com-ing to take me some glo - ri - ous day,

CHORUS

I've a peace that has come there to stay! Con - - - stant-ly a-
Bless-ed Je - sus, how glo-rious Thou art!
O - ver there to my heav-en-ly home! Con-stant-ly a - bid - ing,

bid - - - ing, Je - - - sus is mine; . . .
con-stant-ly a - bid - ing, Je - sus is mine, yes, Je - sus is mine;

Con - - - stant-ly a - bid - - - ing, rap - ture di-
Con-stant-ly a - bid - ing, con-stant-ly a - bid-ing, rap-ture di-vine, O

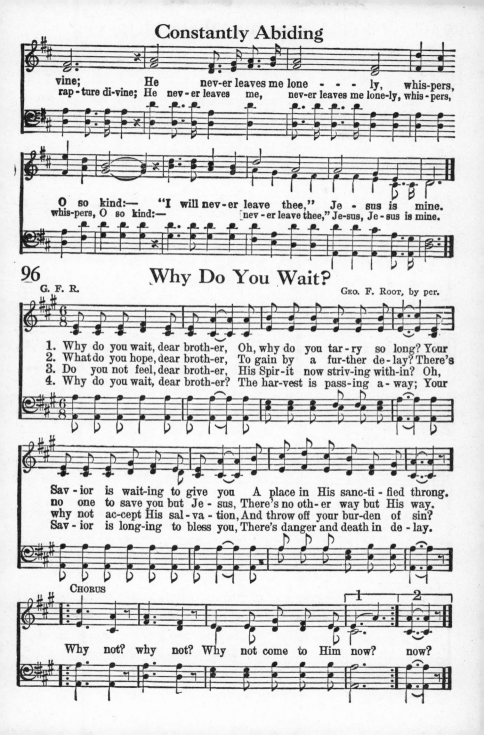

97 I'll Go Where You Want Me to Go

MARY BROWN

CARRIE E. ROUNSEFELL

1. It may not be on the mountain height, Or o - ver the storm - y sea,
2. Perhaps to - day there are lov - ing words Which Jesus would have me speak;
3. There's surely somewhere a low - ly place In earth's harvest fields so wide,

It may not be at the bat - tle's front My Lord will have need of me;
There may be now in the paths of sin Some wand'rer whom I should seek:
Where I may la - bor thro' life's short day For Je - sus, the Cru - ci - fied;

But if, by a still, small voice He calls To paths that I do not know,
O Sav - ior, if Thou wilt be my guide, Tho' dark and rug - ged the way,
So trust - ing my all to Thy ten - der care, And knowing Thou lov - est me,

I'll answer, dear Lord, with my hand in Thine, I'll go where you want me to go.
My voice shall ech - o the mes - sage sweet, I'll say what you want me to say.
I'll do Thy will with a heart sin - cere, I'll be what you want me to be.

REFRAIN

I'll go where you want me to go, dear Lord, Over mountain, or plain, or sea;

I'll Go Where You Want Me to Go

I'll say what you want me to say, dear Lord, I'll be what you want me to be.

98 He Lifted Me

CHARLOTTE G. HOMER   CHAS. H. GABRIEL

1. In lov-ing-kind-ness Je-sus came, My soul in mer-cy to re-claim,
2. He called me long be-fore I heard, Be-fore my sin-ful heart was stirred,
3. His brow was pierced with man-y a thorn, His hands by cru-el nails were torn,
4. Now on a high-er plane I dwell, And with my soul I know 'tis well;

And from the depths of sin and shame Thro' grace He lift-ed me. . . . .
But when I took Him at His word, For-giv'n He lift-ed me. . . . .
When from my guilt and grief, for-lorn, In love He lift-ed me. . . . .
Yet how or why, I can-not tell, He should have lift-ed me.

He lift-ed me.

CHORUS

From sink-ing sand He lift-ed me, With ten-der hand He lift-ed me,

From shades of night to planes of light, O praise His name, He lift-ed me!

99 Tell Me the Story of Jesus

FANNY J. CROSBY

JNO. R. SWENEY

1. Tell me the sto - ry of Je - sus, Write on my heart ev - 'ry word;
2. Fast-ing a - lone in the des - ert, Tell of the days that are past,
3. Tell of the cross where they nailed Him, Writh-ing in an-guish and pain;

CHO.—*Tell me the sto - ry of Je - sus, Write on my heart ev - 'ry word;*

FINE

Tell me the sto - ry most pre - cious, Sweet-est that ev - er was heard.
How for our sins He was tempt - ed, Yet was tri - um-phant at last.
Tell of the grave where they laid Him, Tell how He liv - eth a - gain.

Tell me the sto - ry most pre - cious, Sweet - est that ev - er was heard.

Tell how the an - gels, in cho - rus, Sang as they welcomed His birth,
Tell of the years of His la - bor, Tell of the sor - row He bore,
Love in that sto - ry so ten - der, Clear - er than ev - er I see:

D. C. for Chorus

"Glo - ry to God in the high - est! Peace and good ti - dings to earth."
He was de-spised and af - flict - ed, Home-less, de - ject - ed and poor.
Stay, let me weep while you whis - per, Love paid the ran - som for me.

100 I Love to Tell the Story

KATHERINE HANKEY

WILLIAM G. FISCHER

1. I love to tell the sto - ry Of un - seen things a - bove, Of Je - sus
2. I love to tell the sto - ry; More won - der - ful it seems Than all the
3. I love to tell the sto - ry; 'Tis pleas-ant to re - peat What seems each
4. I love to tell the sto - ry; For those who know it best Seem hun - ger -

and His glo - ry, Of Je - sus and His love, I love to tell the sto - ry,
gold - en fan-cies Of all my golden dreams. I love to tell the sto - ry,
time I tell it, More won-der-ful - ly sweet. I love to tell the sto - ry;
ing and thirsting To hear it like the rest. And when, in scenes of glo - ry,

Because I know 'tis true, It sat - is-fies my longings, As nothing else can do.
It did so much for me; And that is just the rea-son I tell it now to thee
For some have never heard The message of salvation From God's own holy word.
I sing the new, new song, 'Twill be the old, old story, That I have loved so long.

CHORUS

I love to tell the sto - ry! 'Twill be my theme in glo - ry

To tell the old, old sto - ry Of Je - sus and His love.

Blessed Assurance

FANNY J. CROSBY

MRS. JOS. F. KNAPP

1. Bless-ed as - sur - ance, Je - sus is mine! O what a fore-taste of
2. Per - fect sub-mis - sion, per-fect de - light, Vi-sions of rap-ture now
3. Per - fect sub-mis - sion, all is at rest, I in my Sav - ior am

glo - ry di - vine! Heir of sal - va - tion, purchase of God, Born of His
burst on my sight! Angels de-scend-ing, bring from a - bove Ech-oes of
hap - py and blest; Watching and waiting, look-ing a - bove, Filled with His

Spir - it, washed in His blood.
mer - cy, whis-pers of love.   CHORUS   This is my sto - ry, this is my
good - ness, lost in His love.

song, Prais-ing my Sav - ior all the day long; This is my

sto - ry, this is my song, Praising my Sav - ior all the day long.

Jesus Is Calling

Fanny J. Crosby

Geo. C. Stebbins

1. Je-sus is ten-der-ly call-ing thee home—Call-ing to-day,
2. Je-sus is call-ing the wea-ry to rest— Call-ing to-day,
3. Je-sus is wait-ing; O come to Him now— Wait-ing to-day,
4. Je-sus is plead-ing; O list to His voice: Hear Him to-day,

call-ing to-day; Why from the sun-shine of love wilt thou roam
call-ing to-day; Bring Him thy bur-den and thou shalt be blest:
wait-ing to-day; Come with thy sins; at His feet low-ly bow;
hear Him to-day; They who be-lieve on His name shall re-joice;

Far-ther and far-ther a - way?
He will not turn thee a - way.
Come, and no lon-ger de - lay.
Quick-ly a-rise and a - way.

REFRAIN

Call - - ing to-day, ...
Call - ing, call-ing to-day, to-day,

Call - - ing to - day, ...
Call - ing, call-ing to - day, to - day,

Je - - - - sus is
Je - sus is ten - der - ly

call - - - ing, is ten-der-ly call-ing to-day.
call-ing to-day,

I Am Thine, O Lord

F. J. CROSBY   W. H. DOANE

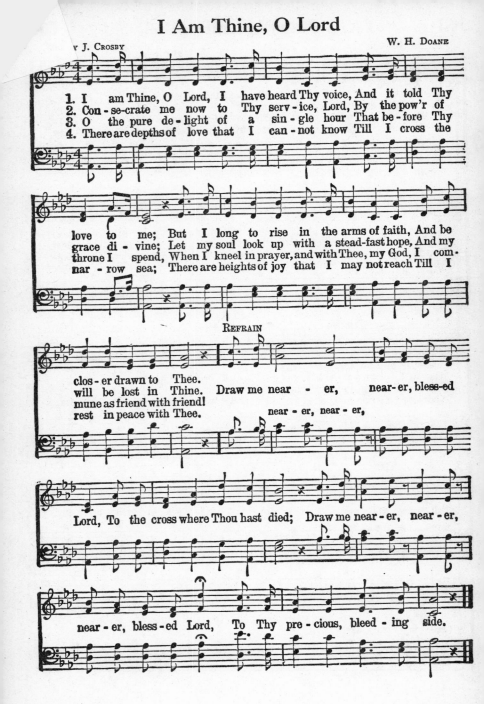

1. I am Thine, O Lord, I have heard Thy voice, And it told Thy
2. Con-se-crate me now to Thy serv-ice, Lord, By the pow'r of
3. O the pure de-light of a sin-gle hour That be-fore Thy
4. There are depths of love that I can-not know Till I cross the

love to me; But I long to rise in the arms of faith, And be
grace di-vine; Let my soul look up with a stead-fast hope, And my
throne I spend, When I kneel in prayer, and with Thee, my God, I com-
nar-row sea; There are heights of joy that I may not reach Till I

REFRAIN

clos-er drawn to Thee.
will be lost in Thine.   Draw me near - er,   near-er, bless-ed
mune as friend with friend!
rest in peace with Thee.   near - er, near - er,

Lord, To the cross where Thou hast died; Draw me near-er, near-er,

near-er, bless-ed Lord, To Thy pre-cious, bleed-ing side.

I Know Whom I Have Believed

El Nathan
Moderato

James McGranahan

1. I know not why God's won-drous grace To me He hath made known,
2. I know not how this sav-ing faith To me He did im-part,
3. I know not how the Spir-it moves, Con-vinc-ing men of sin,
4. I know not what of good or ill May be re-served for me,
5. I know not when my Lord may come, At night or noon-day fair,

Nor why un-wor-thy—Christ in love Re-deemed me for His own.
Nor how be-liev-ing in His Word Wrought peace within my heart.
Re-veal-ing Je-sus thro' the Word, Cre-at-ing faith in Him.
Of wea-ry ways or gold-en days, Be-fore His face I see.
Nor if I walk the vale with Him, Or "meet Him in the air."

CHORUS

But "I know whom I have be-liev-ed, and am per-suad-ed that He is

a-ble To keep that which I've committed Un-to Him a-gainst that day."

105 Higher Ground

JOHNSON OATMAN, JR.

CHAS. H. GABRIEL

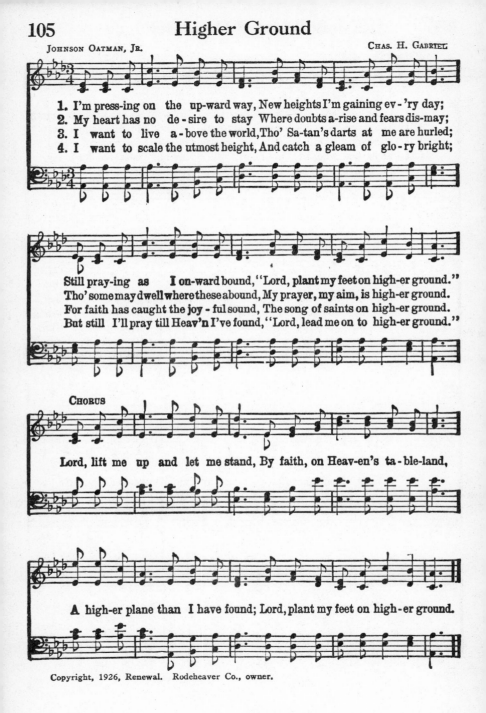

1. I'm press-ing on the up-ward way, New heights I'm gaining ev-'ry day;
2. My heart has no de-sire to stay Where doubts a-rise and fears dis-may;
3. I want to live a-bove the world, Tho' Sa-tan's darts at me are hurled;
4. I want to scale the utmost height, And catch a gleam of glo-ry bright;

Still pray-ing as I on-ward bound, "Lord, plant my feet on high-er ground."
Tho' some may dwell where these abound, My prayer, my aim, is high-er ground.
For faith has caught the joy-ful sound, The song of saints on high-er ground.
But still I'll pray till Heav'n I've found, "Lord, lead me on to high-er ground."

CHORUS

Lord, lift me up and let me stand, By faith, on Heav-en's ta-ble-land,

A high-er plane than I have found; Lord, plant my feet on high-er ground.

106 Softly and Tenderly

W. L. T.

WILL L. THOMPSON

Very slow **pp**

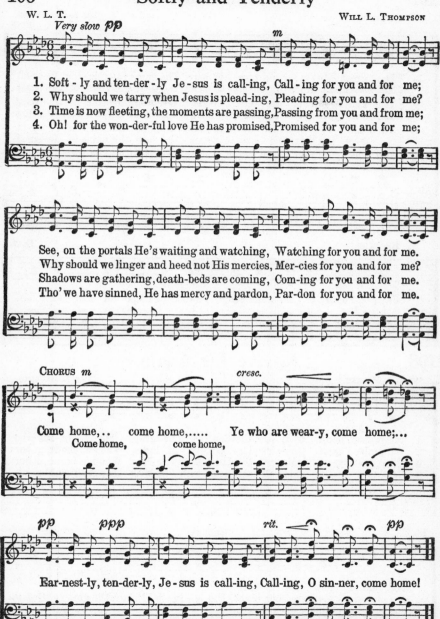

1. Soft - ly and ten-der-ly Je-sus is call-ing, Call-ing for you and for me;
2. Why should we tarry when Jesus is plead-ing, Pleading for you and for me?
3. Time is now fleeting, the moments are passing, Passing from you and from me;
4. Oh! for the won-der-ful love He has promised, Promised for you and for me;

See, on the portals He's waiting and watching, Watching for you and for me.
Why should we linger and heed not His mercies, Mer-cies for you and for me?
Shadows are gathering, death-beds are coming, Com-ing for you and for me.
Tho' we have sinned, He has mercy and pardon, Par-don for you and for me.

CHORUS *m*　　　　*cresc.*

Come home,.. come home,...... Ye who are wear-y, come home;...
Come home,　　come home,

pp　　**ppp**　　　　　*rit.*　　**pp**

Ear-nest-ly, ten-der-ly, Je-sus is call-ing, Call-ing, O sin-ner, come home!

107 **The Great Physician**

WM. HUNTER

J. H. STOCKTON
FINE

1. {The great Phy-si-cian now is here, The sym-pa-thiz-ing Je-sus;
   {He speaks the droop-ing heart to cheer, O hear the voice of Je-sus.

2. {Your man-y sins are all for-giv'n, O hear the voice of Je-sus;
   {Go on your way in peace to heav'n, And wear a crown with Je-sus.

3. {All glo-ry to the dy-ing Lamb! I now be-lieve in Je-sus;
   {I love the bless-ed Sav-ior's name, I love the name of Je-sus.

4. {And when to that bright world a-bove, We rise to be with Je-sus,
   {We'll sing a-round the throne of love, His name, the name of Je-sus.

D. S.—*Sweet-est car-ol ev-er sung,   Je-sus, bless-ed Je-sus.*

REFRAIN
D. S.

Sweet-est note of ser-aph song, Sweet-est name on mor-tal tongue;

108 **Revive Us Again**

WM. P. MACKAY

JOHN J. HUSBAND

1. We praise Thee, O God! for the Son of Thy love, For Je-sus who
2. We praise Thee, O God! for Thy Spir-it of light, Who has shown us our
3. All glo-ry and praise to the Lamb that was slain, Who has borne all our
4. Re-vive us a-gain; fill each heart with Thy love; May each soul be re-

CHORUS

died, and is now gone a-bove.
Sav-ior, and scat-tered our night. Hal-le-lu-jah! Thine the glo-ry, Hal-le-
sins, and has cleansed ev-'ry stain.
kin-dled with fire from a-bove.

Revive Us Again

lu - jah! a - men; Hal - le - lu - jah! Thine the glo - ry, re - vive us a - gain.

109 What a Friend

JOSEPH SCRIVEN   CHARLES C. CONVERSE

1. What a Friend we have in Je - sus, All our sins and griefs to bear!
2. Have we tri - als and temp - ta - tions? Is there troub-le an - y - where?
3. Are we weak and heav-y - la - den, Cumbered with a load of care?—

What a priv - i - lege to car - ry Ev - 'ry-thing to God in prayer!
We should nev-er be dis - cour-aged, Take it to the Lord in prayer.
Pre - cious Sav-ior, still our ref - uge,—Take it to the Lord in prayer.

O what peace we oft - en for - feit, O what need-less pain we bear,
Can we find a friend so faith - ful Who will all our sor-rows share?
Do thy friends despise, for-sake thee? Take it to the Lord in prayer;

All be-cause we do not car - ry Ev - 'ry-thing to God in prayer!
Je - sus knows our ev - 'ry weak - ness, Take it to the Lord in prayer.
In His arms He'll take and shield thee, Thou wilt find a sol - ace there.

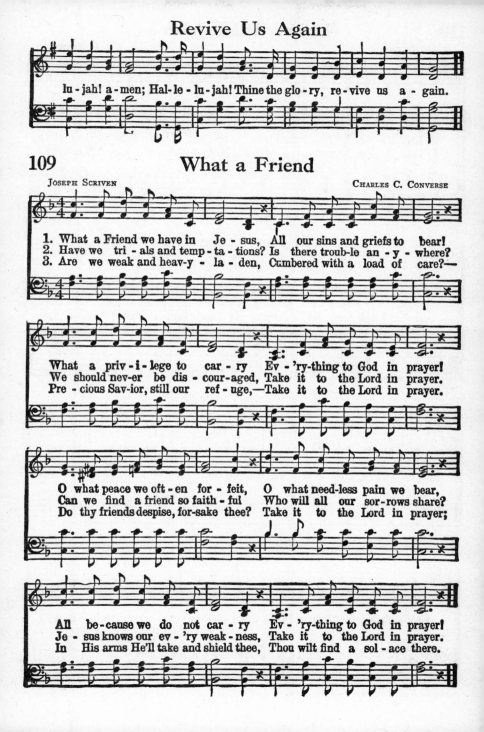

110 Whiter Than Snow

JAMES NICHOLSON

WM. G. FISCHER

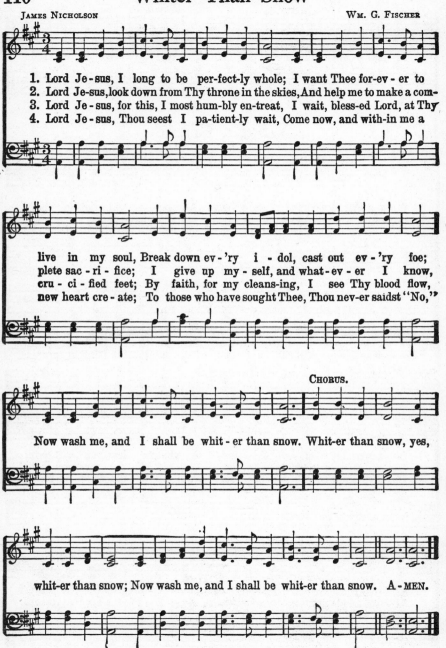

1. Lord Je-sus, I long to be per-fect-ly whole; I want Thee for-ev-er to
2. Lord Je-sus, look down from Thy throne in the skies, And help me to make a com-
3. Lord Je-sus, for this, I most hum-bly en-treat, I wait, bless-ed Lord, at Thy
4. Lord Je-sus, Thou seest I pa-tient-ly wait, Come now, and with-in me a

live in my soul, Break down ev-'ry i-dol, cast out ev-'ry foe;
plete sac-ri-fice; I give up my-self, and what-ev-er I know,
cru-ci-fied feet; By faith, for my cleans-ing, I see Thy blood flow,
new heart cre-ate; To those who have sought Thee, Thou nev-er saidst "No,"

CHORUS.

Now wash me, and I shall be whit-er than snow. Whit-er than snow, yes,

whit-er than snow; Now wash me, and I shall be whit-er than snow. A-MEN.

111 My Hope Is Built

EDWARD MOTE

WILLIAM B. BRADBURY

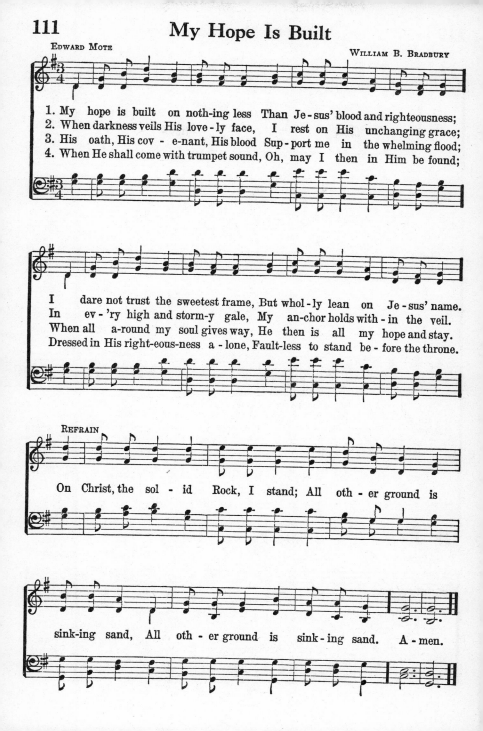

1. My hope is built on noth-ing less Than Je-sus' blood and righteousness;
2. When darkness veils His love-ly face, I rest on His unchanging grace;
3. His oath, His cov - e-nant, His blood Sup-port me in the whelming flood;
4. When He shall come with trumpet sound, Oh, may I then in Him be found;

I dare not trust the sweetest frame, But whol-ly lean on Je-sus' name.
In ev-'ry high and storm-y gale, My an-chor holds with-in the veil.
When all a-round my soul gives way, He then is all my hope and stay.
Dressed in His right-eous-ness a-lone, Fault-less to stand be-fore the throne.

REFRAIN

On Christ, the sol - id Rock, I stand; All oth - er ground is

sink-ing sand, All oth - er ground is sink-ing sand. A - men.

112 Almost Persuaded

P. P. B.
P. P. BLISS

1. "Al - most per-suad - ed," now to be - lieve; "Al - most per-suad - ed,"
2. "Al - most per-suad - ed," come, come to - day; "Al - most per-suad - ed,"
3. "Al - most per-suad - ed," har - vest is past! "Al - most per-suad - ed,"

Christ to re - ceive; Seems now some soul to say, "Go, Spir - it,
turn not a - way; Je - sus in - vites you here, An - gels are
doom comes at last! "Al - most" can - not a - vail; "Al - most" is

go Thy way, Some more con - ven - ient day On Thee I'll call."
lin-g'ring near, Prayers rise from hearts so dear, O wan-d'rer, come.
but to fail! Sad, sad, that bit - ter wail, "Al - most," but lost!

113 Jesus Never Fails

A. A. LUTHER Copyright, 1927, by Mrs. O. E. Williams. Used by permission. A. A. LUTHER

1. Earth-ly friends may prove untrue, Doubts and fears as-sail; One still loves and
2. Tho' the sky be dark and drear, Fierce and strong the gale, Just re-mem-ber
3. In life's dark and bit - ter hour Love will still pre - vail; Trust His ev - er-

Jesus Never Fails

CHORUS

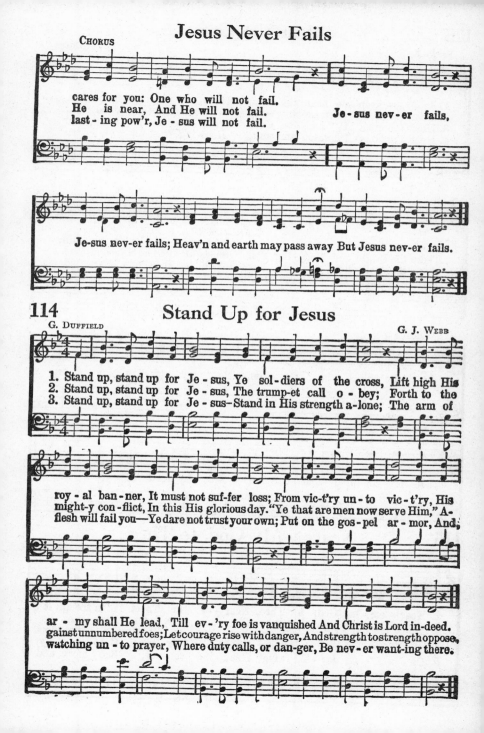

cares for you: One who will not fail.
He is near, And He will not fail.
last - ing pow'r, Je - sus will not fail.

Je - sus nev - er fails,

Je-sus nev-er fails; Heav'n and earth may pass away But Jesus nev-er fails.

114 Stand Up for Jesus

G. DUFFIELD

G. J. WEBB

1. Stand up, stand up for Je - sus, Ye sol - diers of the cross, Lift high His
2. Stand up, stand up for Je - sus, The trump-et call o - bey; Forth to the
3. Stand up, stand up for Je - sus—Stand in His strength a-lone; The arm of

roy - al ban - ner, It must not suf-fer loss; From vic-t'ry un - to vic-t'ry, His
might-y con-flict, In this His glorious day. "Ye that are men now serve Him," A-
flesh will fail you—Ye dare not trust your own; Put on the gos-pel ar-mor, And,

ar - my shall He lead, Till ev - 'ry foe is vanquished And Christ is Lord in-deed.
gainst unnumbered foes; Let courage rise with danger, And strength to strength oppose,
watching un - to prayer, Where duty calls, or dan-ger, Be nev - er want-ing there.

Near the Cross

FANNY J. CROSBY

W. H. DOANE

1. Je - sus, keep me near the cross, There a pre - cious foun - tain
2. Near the cross, a trem-bling soul, Love and mer - cy found me;
3. Near the cross! O Lamb of God, Bring its scenes be - fore me;
4. Near the cross I'll watch and wait, Hop - ing, trust-ing ev - er,

Free to all— a heal - ing stream, Flows from Cal-v'ry's moun - tain.
There the Bright and Morn-ing Star Sheds its beams a - round me.
Help me walk from day to day, With its shad-ows o'er me.
Till I reach the gold - en strand, Just be - yond the riv - er.

CHORUS

In the cross, in the cross, Be my glo - ry ev - er;

Till my rap-tured soul shall find Rest be - yond the riv - er.

Nearer, My God, to Thee

SARAH F. ADAMS

Arr. by LOWELL MASON

1. Near - er, my God, to Thee, Near - er to Thee! E'en though it
2. Though like the wan - der - er, The sun gone down, Dark-ness be
3. There let the way ap - pear, Steps un - to Heav'n: All that Thou
4. Then, with my wak - ing tho'ts Bright with Thy praise, Out of my
5. Or if on joy - ful wing, Cleav - ing the sky, Sun, moon, and

Nearer, My God, to Thee

be a cross That rais-eth me; Still all my song shall be,
o-ver me, My rest a stone; Yet in my dreams I'd be
send-est me, In mer-cy giv'n: An-gels to beck-on me,
sto-ny griefs Beth-el I'll raise; So by my woes to be
stars for-got, Up-wards I'll fly, Still all my song shall be,

Near-er, my God, to Thee, Near-er, my God, to Thee, Near-er to Thee!

117 Jesus, Lover of My Soul

Charles Wesley

S. B. Marsh
Fine

1. { Je - sus, Lov - er of my soul, Let me to Thy bos - om fly,
{ While the near - er wa - ters roll, While the tem-pest still is high!

2. { Oth - er ref - uge have I none; Hangs my help-less soul on Thee:
{ Leave, ah, leave me not a - lone, Still sup-port and com - fort me!

3. { Thou, O Christ, art all I want; More than all in Thee I find;
{ Raise the fall - en, cheer the faint, Heal the sick, and lead the blind.

4. { Plenteous grace with Thee is found, Grace to cov - er all my sin;
{ Let the heal-ing streams a-bound, Make and keep me pure with - in.

D.C.—Safe in-to the ha - ven guide, O re-ceive my soul at last!
D.C.—Cov - er my de-fense-less head With the shad-ow of Thy wing.
D.C.—False and full of sin I am, Thou art full of truth and grace.
D.C.—Spring Thou up with-in my heart, Rise to all e - ter - ni - ty.

D.C.

Hide me, O my Sav - ior, hide, Till the storm of life is past;
All my trust on Thee is stayed, All my help from Thee I bring;
Just and ho - ly is Thy name, I am all un-right-eous - ness;
Thou of life the foun-tain art; Free-ly let me take of Thee;

118 Bringing In the Sheaves

KNOWLES SHAW

GEORGE A. MINOR

1. Sow-ing in the morn-ing, sow-ing seeds of kind-ness, Sow-ing in the
2. Sow-ing in the sun-shine, sow-ing in the shad-ows, Fear-ing nei-ther
3. Go-ing forth with weep-ing, sow-ing for the Mas-ter, Tho' the loss sus-

noon-tide and the dew-y eve; Wait-ing for the har-vest,
clouds nor win-ter's chill-ing breeze; By and by the har-vest,
tained our spir-it oft-en grieves; When our weep-ing's o-ver,

and the time of reap-ing, We shall come re-joic-ing, bring-ing in the sheaves.
and the la-bor end-ed, We shall come re-joic-ing, bring-ing in the sheaves.
He will bid us wel-come, We shall come re-joic-ing, bring-ing in the sheaves.

CHORUS

Bring-ing in the sheaves, bring-ing in the sheaves, We shall come re-joic-
Bring-ing in the sheaves, bring-ing in the sheaves, We shall come re-joic-

1. ing, bring-ing in the sheaves; 2. ing, bring-ing in the sheaves.

119 Saved, Saved!

J. P. S.

J. P. Scholfield

1. I've found a friend who is all to me,.... His
2. He saves me from ev-'ry sin and harm,. Se-
3. When poor and need-y and all a-lone,.... In

love is ev-er true;...... I love to tell how He
cures my soul each day;...... I'm lean-ing strong on His
love He said to me,........ "Come un-to me and I'll

lift-ed me.... And what His grace can do for you...
might-y arm;.. I know He'll guide me all the way...
lead you home, To live with me e-ter-nal-ly."...

CHORUS.

Saved .... by His pow'r di-vine, Saved .... to new life sub-lime!
Saved by His pow'r,   Saved to new life,

rit.

Life now is sweet and my joy is com-plete, For I'm Saved, saved, saved!

120 More Love to Thee

ELIZABETH PRENTISS

W. H. DOANE

1. More love to Thee, O Christ, More love to Thee! Hear Thou the
2. Once earth-ly joy I craved, Sought peace and rest; Now Thee a-
3. Then shall my lat-est breath Whis-per Thy praise; This be the

pray'r I make On bend-ed knee; This is my earn-est plea:
lone I seek, Give what is best; This all my pray'r shall be:
part-ing cry My heart shall raise; This still its pray'r shall be:

More love, O Christ, to Thee, More love to Thee, More love to Thee!

121 I Am Coming, Lord

L. H.

L. HARTSOUGH

1. I hear Thy welcome voice, That calls me, Lord, to Thee, For cleansing in Thy
2. Tho' coming weak and vile, Thou dost my strength assure; Thou dost my vileness
3. 'Tis Je-sus calls me on To per-fect faith and love, To per-fect hope, and

CHORUS

pre-cious blood That flowed on Cal-va-ry.
full-y cleanse, Till spot-less all and pure.   I am coming, Lord! Coming now to
peace, and trust, For earth and Heav'n above.

I Am Coming, Lord

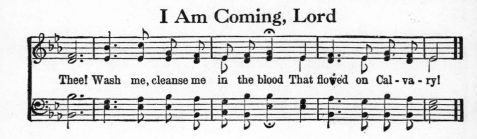

Thee! Wash me, cleanse me in the blood That flowed on Cal-va-ry!

122 I Would Be True

HOWARD ARNOLD WALTER

JOSEPH YATES PEEK

1. I would be true, for there are those who trust me; I would be
2. I would be friend of all— the foe, the friend-less; I would be

pure, for there are those who care; I would be strong, for
giv-ing, and for-get the gift; I would be hum-ble,

there is much to suf-fer; I would be brave, for there is much to
for I know my weak-ness; I would look up, and laugh, and love, and

dare, I would be brave, for there is much to dare.
lift, I would look up, and laugh, and love, and lift.

123 Jesus, Savior, Pilot Me

EDWARD HOPPER

J. E. GOULD

1. Je - sus, Sav - ior, pi - lot me O - ver life's tem - pes-tuous sea:
2. As a moth - er stills her child, Thou canst hush the o - cean wild;
3. When at last I near the shore, And the fear - ful break-ers roar

D. C.—Chart and com-pass come from Thee, Je - sus, Sav - ior, pi - lot me.
D. C.—Won-drous Sov-'reign of the sea, Je - sus, Sav - ior, pi - lot me.
D. C.—May I hear Thee say to me, "Fear not, I will pi - lot thee."

Un-known waves be - fore me roll, Hid - ing rocks and treach'rous shoal;
Bois-t'rous waves o - bey Thy will When Thou say'st to them "Be still!"
'Twixt me and the peace-ful rest, Then, while lean-ing on Thy breast,

124 I Need Thee Every Hour

MRS. ANNIE S. HAWKS

REV. ROBERT LOWRY

1. I need Thee ev - 'ry hour, Most gra-cious Lord; No ten - der voice like
2. I need Thee ev - 'ry hour, Stay Thou near by; Temp-ta - tions lose their
3. I need Thee ev - 'ry hour, In joy or pain; Come quick-ly and a -
4. I need Thee ev - 'ry hour, Most Ho - ly One; O make me Thine in -

CHORUS

Thine Can peace af - ford.
pow'r When Thou art nigh. I need Thee, O I need Thee; Ev - 'ry hour I
bide, Or life is vain.
deed, Thou bless-ed Son!

I Need Thee Every Hour

need Thee! O bless me now, my Sav-ior, I come to Thee!

125   Sweet Hour of Prayer

W. W. WALFORD
WM. B. BRADBURY

1. Sweet hour of pray'r! sweet hour of pray'r! That calls me from a world of care,
2. Sweet hour of pray'r! sweet hour of pray'r! Thy wings shall my pe-ti-tion bear
3. Sweet hour of pray'r! sweet hour of pray'r! May I thy con-so-la-tion share,

And bids me at my Father's throne Make all my wants and wish-es known;
To Him whose truth and faith-ful-ness En-gage the wait-ing soul to bless;
Till, from Mount Pisgah's loft-y height, I view my home, and take my flight:

In sea-sons of dis-tress and grief, My soul has oft-en found re-lief,
And since He bids me seek His face, Be-lieve His word and trust His grace,
This robe of flesh I'll drop and rise To seize the ev-er-last-ing prize;

And oft escaped the tempter's snare By thy re-turn, sweet hour of pray'r.
I'll cast on Him my ev-'ry care, And wait for thee, sweet hour of pray'r.
And shout, while passing thro' the air, Farewell, farewell, sweet hour of pray'r.

126 Savior, More Than Life

FANNY J. CROSBY

W. H. DOANE

1. Sav - ior, more than life to me, I am clinging, clinging close to Thee;
2. Thro' this changing world be-low, Lead me gen-tly, gen-tly as I go;
3. Let me love Thee more and more, Till this fleet-ing, fleet-ing life is o'er;

Let Thy pre-cious blood ap-plied, Keep me ev - er, ev - er near Thy side.
Trusting Thee, I can - not stray, I can nev-er, nev-er lose my way.
Till my soul is lost in love, In a brighter, brighter world a - bove.

Fine

D.S.—*May Thy ten - der love to me Bind me clo - ser, clo - ser, Lord, to Thee.*

REFRAIN

D. S.

Ev - 'ry day, ev - 'ry hour, Let me feel Thy cleansing pow'r;
Ev - 'ry day and hour, ev - 'ry day and hour,

127 Glory to His Name

Rev. E. A. HOFFMAN

Rev. J. H. STOCKTON

1. Down at the cross where my Sav - ior died, Down where for cleansing from
2. I am so won-drous-ly saved from sin, Je - sus so sweet-ly a-
3. Oh, pre-cious foun-tain that saves from sin, I am so glad I have
4. Come to this foun-tain so rich and sweet; Cast thy poor soul at the

Glory to His Name

sin I cried, There to my heart was the blood ap-plied; Glo-ry to His name.
bides with-in, There at the cross where He took me in; Glo-ry to His name.
en - tered in; There Jesus saves me and keeps me clean; Glo-ry to His name.
Sav-ior's feet; Plunge in to-day, and be made com-plete; Glo-ry to His name.

D. S.—*There to my heart was the blood ap-plied; Glo-ry to His name.*

CHORUS

D. S.

Glo - ry to His name,... Glo - ry to His name;...

128 Fairest Lord Jesus

CRUSADERS' HYMN

ARR. BY RICHARD S. WILLIS

1. Fair - est Lord Je - sus! Rul - er of all na - ture!
2. Fair are the mead - ows, Fair - er still the wood - lands,
3. Fair is the sun - shine, Fair - er still the moon - light,

O Thou of God and man the Son! Thee will I cher - ish,
Robed in the bloom - ing garb of spring; Je - sus is fair - er,
And all the twin - kling star - ry host; Je - sus shines bright - er,

Thee will I hon - or, Thou, my soul's glo - ry, joy, and crown!
Je - sus is pur - er, Who makes the woe - ful heart to sing!
Je - sus shines pur - er, Than all the an - gels heav'n can boast!

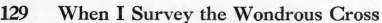

129 When I Survey the Wondrous Cross

ISAAC WATTS   HAMBURG. L. M.   Arr. by LOWELL MASON

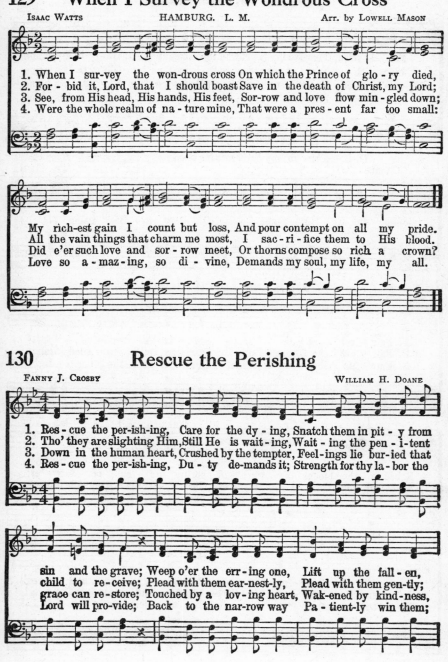

1. When I sur-vey the won-drous cross On which the Prince of glo-ry died,
2. For - bid it, Lord, that I should boast Save in the death of Christ, my Lord;
3. See, from His head, His hands, His feet, Sor-row and love flow min-gled down:
4. Were the whole realm of na-ture mine, That were a pres-ent far too small:

My rich-est gain I count but loss, And pour contempt on all my pride.
All the vain things that charm me most, I sac-ri-fice them to His blood.
Did e'er such love and sor - row meet, Or thorns compose so rich a crown?
Love so a-maz-ing, so di - vine, Demands my soul, my life, my all.

130 Rescue the Perishing

FANNY J. CROSBY   WILLIAM H. DOANE

1. Res - cue the per-ish-ing, Care for the dy - ing, Snatch them in pit - y from
2. Tho' they are slighting Him, Still He is wait-ing, Wait - ing the pen - i-tent
3. Down in the human heart, Crushed by the tempter, Feel-ings lie bur-ied that
4. Res - cue the per-ish-ing, Du - ty de-mands it; Strength for thy la-bor the

sin and the grave; Weep o'er the err - ing one, Lift up the fall - en,
child to re-ceive; Plead with them ear-nest-ly, Plead with them gen-tly;
grace can re-store; Touched by a lov-ing heart, Wak-ened by kind-ness,
Lord will pro-vide; Back to the nar-row way Pa - tient-ly win them;

Rescue the Perishing

Tell them of Je-sus the might-y to save.
He will for-give if they on-ly be-lieve. Res-cue the per-ish-ing,
Chords that are bro-ken will vi-brate once more.
Tell the poor wan-d'rer a Sav-ior has died.

Care for the dy-ing; Je-sus is mer-ci-ful, Je-sus will save.

131 Footsteps of Jesus

MARY B. C. SLADE   A. B. EVERETT

1. Sweet-ly, Lord, have we heard Thee call-ing, Come, fol-low Me!
2. Tho' they lead o'er the cold, dark mountains, Seek-ing His sheep;
3. If they lead thro' the tem-ple ho-ly, Preach-ing the word;
4. Then at last, when on high He sees us, Our jour-ney done,

FINE

And we see where Thy foot-prints fall-ing Lead us to Thee.
Or a-long by Si-lo-am's foun-tains, Help-ing the weak:
Or in homes of the poor and low-ly, Serv-ing the Lord:
We will rest where the steps of Je-sus End at His throne.

D.S.—*We will fol-low the steps of Je-sus wher-e'er they go.*

CHORUS   D. S.

Foot-prints of Je-sus, that make the path-way glow;

132 How Sweet the Name of Jesus Sounds

ST. PETER'S, OXFORD. C. M.

John Newton   Alexander R. Reinagle

1. How sweet the name of Je - sus sounds In a be - liev - er's ear! It
2. It makes the wound-ed spir - it whole, And calms the trou-bled breast, 'Tis
3. Dear name! the Rock on which I build, My shield and hid - ing place; My
4. Weak is the ef - fort of my heart, And cold my warmest thought; But
5. Till then, I would Thy love pro-claim With ev - 'ry fleet - ing breath; And

soothes his sor-rows, heals his wounds, And drives a - way his fear.
man - na to the hun - gry soul, And to the wea - ry, rest.
nev - er - fail - ing treas-ury, filled With boundless stores of grace!
when I see Thee as Thou art, I'll praise Thee as I ought.
may the mu - sic of Thy name Refresh my soul in death.   A-men.

133 Take the Name of Jesus With You

Mrs. Lydia Baxter   W. H. Doane

1. Take the name of Je - sus with you, Child of sor - row and of woe;
2. Take the name of Je - sus ev - er, As a shield from ev - 'ry snare;
3. O the precious name of Je - sus! How it thrills our souls with joy,
4. At the name of Je - sus bow - ing, Fall - ing pros-trate at His feet,

It will joy and com-fort give you, Take it, then, where'er you go.
If temp - ta-tions 'round you gath-er, Breathe that ho - ly name in pray'r.
When His lov - ing arms re - ceive us, And His songs our tongues employ!
King of kings in heav'n we'll crown Him, When our jour-ney is com-plete.

Take the Name of Jesus With You

CHORUS

Precious name,   O how sweet!   Hope of earth and joy   of heav'n;

Precious name,   O how sweet!

Precious name,   O how sweet!... Hope of earth and joy   of heav'n.

Precious name, O how sweet, how sweet!

134   Work, for the Night Is Coming

ANNIE L. COGHILL

LOWELL MASON

1. Work, for the night is coming, Work thro' the morning hours; Work while the dew is
2. Work, for the night is coming, Work thro' the sun-ny noon; Fill brightest hours with
3. Work, for the night is coming,   Under the sunset skies; While their bright tints are

sparkling, Work 'mid springing flow'rs; Work when the day grows brighter, Work in the
la - bor, Rest comes sure and soon. Give ev-'ry fly-ing min-ute Something to
glow-ing, Work, for daylight flies. Work till the last beam fad-eth,   Fad-eth to

glow - ing sun; Work, for the night is com-ing, When man's work is done.
keep   in store: Work, for the night is com-ing, When man works no more.
shine no more; Work while the night is dark'ning, When man's work is o'er.

135 Win Them One by One

C. A. M.

C. Austin Miles

In march time

1. If to Christ our on - ly King Men re-deemed we strive to bring,
2. Side by side we stand each day, Saved are we, but lost are they;
3. On - ly cow - ards dare re - fuse, Dare this gift of God mis - use;

Just one way may this be done—We must win them one by one.
They will come if we but dare Speak a word backed up by prayer.
Ere some friend goes to his grave, Speak a word his soul to save.

CHORUS

{ So, you bring the one next to you, And I'll bring the one next to me, In
{ If you'll bring the one next to you, And I bring the one next to me, In

all kinds of weather we'll all work to-geth-er, And see what can be done.

no time at all we'll have them all, So win them, win them one by one.

136 This Is My Father's World

MALTBIE D. BABCOCK

Traditional English Melody
Arranged by FRANKLIN L. SHEPPARD

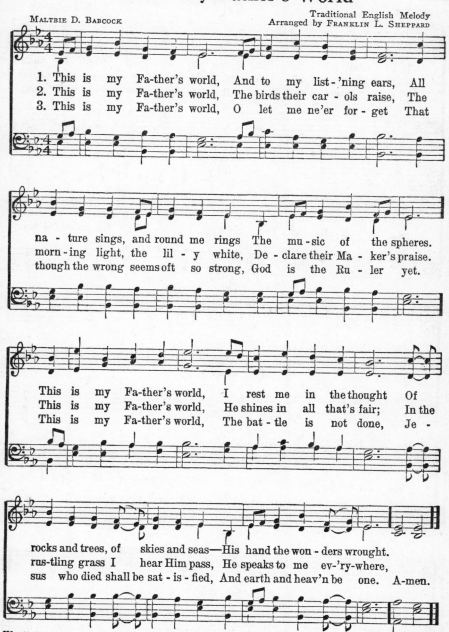

1. This is my Fa-ther's world, And to my list-'ning ears, All
2. This is my Fa-ther's world, The birds their car-ols raise, The
3. This is my Fa-ther's world, O let me ne'er for-get That

na-ture sings, and round me rings The mu-sic of the spheres.
morn-ing light, the lil-y white, De-clare their Ma-ker's praise.
though the wrong seems oft so strong, God is the Ru-ler yet.

This is my Fa-ther's world, I rest me in the thought Of
This is my Fa-ther's world, He shines in all that's fair; In the
This is my Fa-ther's world, The bat-tle is not done, Je-

rocks and trees, of skies and seas—His hand the won-ders wrought.
rus-tling grass I hear Him pass, He speaks to me ev-'ry-where.
sus who died shall be sat-is-fied, And earth and heav'n be one. A-men.

137 I Shall See the King

W. C. POOLE

B. D. ACKLEY

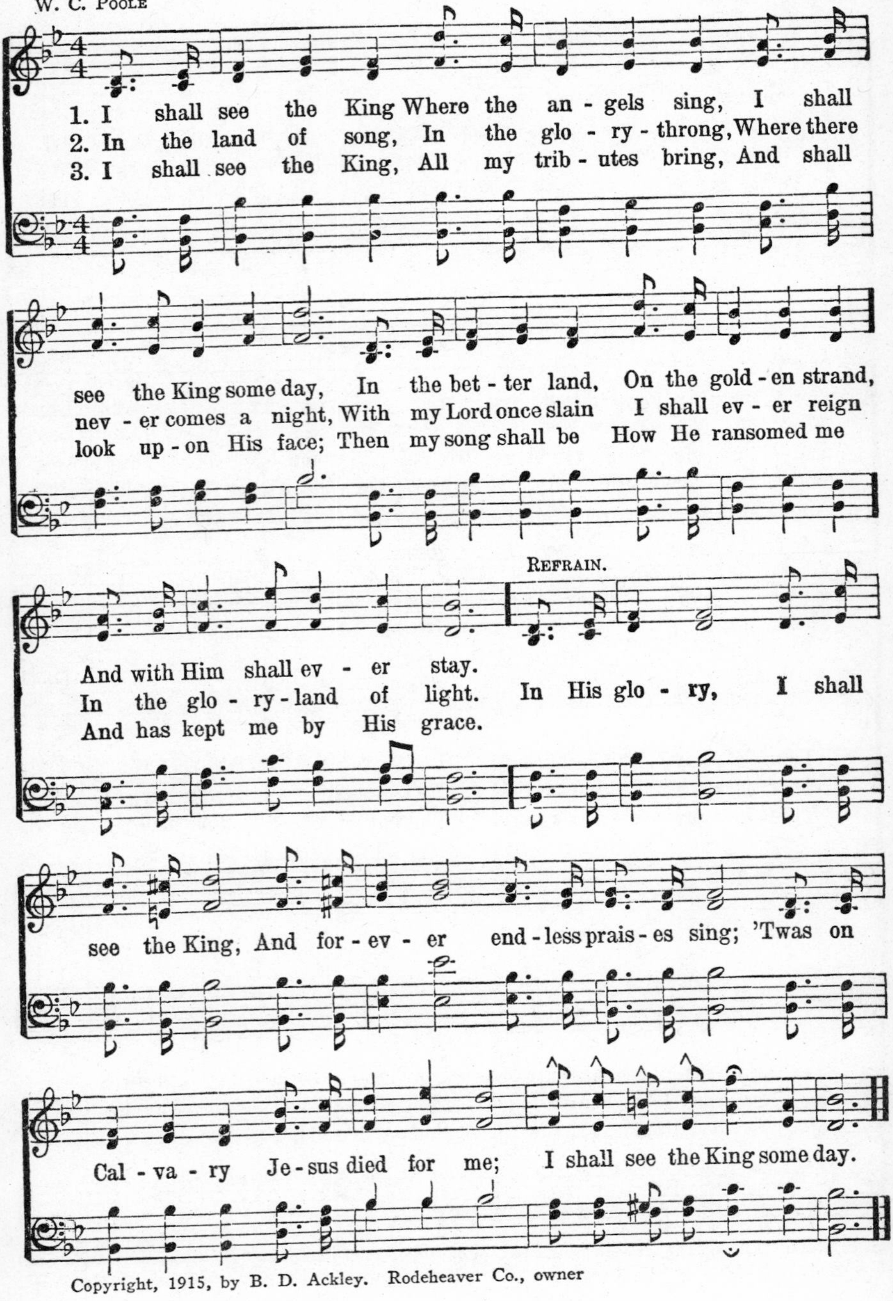

1. I shall see the King Where the an-gels sing, I shall
2. In the land of song, In the glo-ry-throng, Where there
3. I shall see the King, All my trib-utes bring, And shall

see the King some day, In the bet-ter land, On the gold-en strand,
nev-er comes a night, With my Lord once slain I shall ev-er reign
look up-on His face; Then my song shall be How He ransomed me

And with Him shall ev-er stay.
In the glo-ry-land of light.
And has kept me by His grace.

REFRAIN.

In His glo-ry, I shall see the King, And for-ev-er end-less prais-es sing; 'Twas on Cal-va-ry Je-sus died for me; I shall see the King some day.

138 There Is Power in the Blood

L. E. J.

L. E. JONES

1. Would you be free from the bur-den of sin? There's pow'r in the blood,
2. Would you be free from your pas-sion and pride? There's pow'r in the blood,
3. Would you be whit-er, much whiter than snow? There's pow'r in the blood,
4. Would you do serv-ice for Je-sus your King? There's pow'r in the blood,

pow'r in the blood; Would you o'er e-vil a vic-to-ry win? There's
pow'r in the blood; Come for a cleans-ing to Cal-va-ry's tide; There's
pow'r in the blood; Sin-stains are lost in its life-giv-ing flow; There's
pow'r in the blood; Would you live dai-ly His prais-es to sing? There's

CHORUS.

won-der-ful pow'r in the blood. There is pow'r, pow'r, Wonder-working pow'r
there is

In the blood of the Lamb; There is pow'r, pow'r,
In the blood of the Lamb; there is

Won-der-work-ing pow'r In the pre-cious blood of the Lamb.

139 Growing Dearer Each Day

C. H. G.

CHAS. H. GABRIEL

1. How sweet is the love of my Sav-ior! 'Tis boundless and deep as the sea; And
2. I know He is ev-er be-side me! E-ter-ni-ty on-ly will prove The
3. Wher-ev-er He leads I will fol-low, Thro' sor-row, or shadow, or sun; And
4. Some day face to face I shall see Him, And oh, what a joy it will be To

best of it all, it is dai-ly Grow-ing sweet-er and sweet-er to me.
height and the depth of His mercy, And the breadth of His in-fi-nite love.
though I be tried in the fur-nace, I can say, "Lord, Thy will be it done."
know that His love, now so precious, Will for-ev-er grow sweet-er to me.

CHORUS.

Sweet - - er and sweeter to me, ... Dear - - er and
Sweeter to me, grow - ing sweet-er to me, Dear-er each day,

dear-er each day; . . . Oh, won - - der-ful love of my
grow - ing dear-er each day; Oh, won-der-ful love, love of my

Sav - ior, Grow-ing dear - - er each step of my way! A-MEN.
Sav - ior, Grow-ing dear-er and dear-er each step of my way!

140 Follow Me

Rev. George D. Watson
DUET

"TUCKER"
Arr. by George W. Cooke

1. I hear my bless-ed Sav-iour say: "Fol-low Me, fol-low Me, fol-low Me;"
2. "Tho' thou hast sinned, I'll pardon thee, Fol-low Me, fol-low Me, fol-low Me;
3. "Bring un-to Me thy man-y cares, Fol-low Me, fol-low Me, fol-low Me;

His voice is call-ing all the day, "Fol-low Me, fol-low Me, fol-low Me;
From ev-'ry sin I'll set thee free, Fol-low Me, fol-low Me, fol-low Me;
Thy heav-y load My arm up-bears, Fol-low Me, fol-low Me, fol-low Me;

QUARTET

For thee I trod the bit-ter way, ... For thee I gave My life a-way,
In all thy changing life I'll be ..... Thy God, thy guide on land and sea,
Lean on My breast, dismiss thy fears, ... And trust Me thro' thy future years,

the bit-ter way,
thy life I'll be
dis-miss thy fears,

DUET   ad lib.

And drank the gall thy debt to pay, ... Fol-low Me, fol-low Me, fol-low Me."
Thy bliss thro' all e-ter-ni-ty, ... Fol-low Me, fol-low Me, fol-low Me."
My hand shall wipe a-way all tears, ... Fol-low Me, fol-low Me, fol-low Me."

thy debt to pay,
e-ter-ni-ty,
away all tears,

141 All Hail, Immanuel

D. R. van Sickle

Chas. H. Gabriel

1. All hail to Thee, Im-man-u-el, We cast . . . our crowns be-fore Thee;
2. All hail to Thee, Im-man-u-el, The ran - somed hosts surround Thee;
3. All hail to Thee, Im-man-u-el, Our ris - - en King and Sav - ior!

Let ev - 'ry heart o - bey Thy will, And ev - - - 'ry voice a-
And earth - ly mon-archs clam - or forth Their Sov - - 'reign King to
Thy foes are van-quished, and Thou art Om - nip - - - o - tent for-

dore Thee. In praise to Thee, our Sav - ior King, The vi - brant
crown Thee. While those re-deemed in a - ges gone, As - sem - bled
ev - er. Death, sin and hell no lon - ger reign, And Sa - tan's

chords of Heav - en ring, And ech - o back the might-y strain:
round the great white throne, Break forth in - to im - mor - tal song:
pow'r is burst in twain; E - ter - nal glo - ry to Thy Name:

ff

All hail! all hail! All hail! all hail! Im-man-u-ell
All hail! all hail!

All Hail, Immanuel

142 O Jesus, I Have Promised

JOHN E. BODE

ARTHUR H. MANN

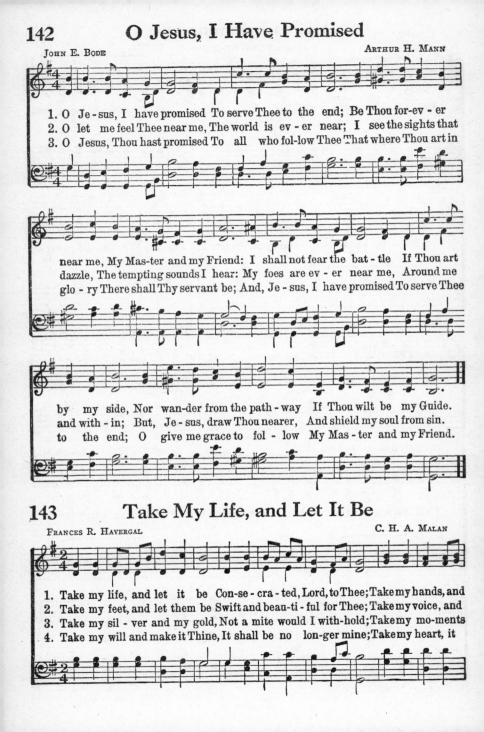

1. O Je - sus, I have promised To serve Thee to the end; Be Thou for-ev - er
2. O let me feel Thee near me, The world is ev - er near; I see the sights that
3. O Jesus, Thou hast promised To all who fol-low Thee That where Thou art in

near me, My Mas-ter and my Friend: I shall not fear the bat - tle If Thou art
dazzle, The tempting sounds I hear: My foes are ev - er near me, Around me
glo - ry There shall Thy servant be; And, Je - sus, I have promised To serve Thee

by my side, Nor wan-der from the path - way If Thou wilt be my Guide.
and with - in; But, Je - sus, draw Thou nearer, And shield my soul from sin.
to the end; O give me grace to fol - low My Mas - ter and my Friend.

143 Take My Life, and Let It Be

FRANCES R. HAVERGAL

C. H. A. MALAN

1. Take my life, and let it be Con-se - cra - ted, Lord, to Thee; Take my hands, and
2. Take my feet, and let them be Swift and beau-ti - ful for Thee; Take my voice, and
3. Take my sil - ver and my gold, Not a mite would I with-hold; Take my mo-ments
4. Take my will and make it Thine, It shall be no lon-ger mine; Take my heart, it

Take My Life, and Let It Be

let them move At the im-pulse of Thy love, At the im-pulse of Thy love.
let me sing Al-ways, on-ly, for my King, Al-ways, on-ly, for my King
and my days. Let them flow in cease-less praise, Let them flow in ceaseless praise
is Thine own. It shall be Thy roy-al throne, It shall be Thy roy-al throne.

144 I Surrender All

J. W. VAN DEVENTER   Copyright, 1895, by Weeden and Van Deventer   W. S. WEEDEN

1. All to Je-sus I sur-ren-der, All to Him I free-ly give;
2. All to Je-sus I sur-ren-der, Hum-bly at His feet I bow,
3. All to Je-sus I sur-ren-der, Make me, Sav-ior, whol-ly Thine;
4. All to Je-sus I sur-ren-der, Lord, I give my-self to Thee;
5. All to Je-sus I sur-ren-der, Now I feel the sa-cred flame;

I will ev-er love and trust Him, In His pres-ence dai-ly live.
World-ly pleas-ures all for-sak-en, Take me, Je-sus, take me now.
Let me feel the Ho-ly Spir-it,—Tru-ly know that Thou art mine.
Fill me with Thy love and pow-er, Let Thy bless-ing fall on me.
Oh, the joy of full sal-va-tion! Glo-ry, glo-ry to His name!

CHORUS

I sur-ren-der all, I sur-ren-der all,
I sur-ren-der all, I sur-ren-der all,

All to Thee, my bless-ed Sav-ior, I sur-ren-der all.

145 God Be With You

J. E. RANKIN

W. G. TOMER

1. God be with you till we meet a-gain; By His counsels guide, uphold you,
2. God be with you till we meet a-gain; 'Neath His wings protecting hide you,
3. God be with you till we meet a-gain; When life's perils thick confound you,
4. God be with you till we meet a-gain; Keep love's banner floating o'er you;

With His sheep se-cure-ly fold you; God be with you till we meet a-gain.
Dai - ly man-na still pro-vide you; God be with you till we meet a-gain.
Put His arms un-fail-ing round you; God be with you till we meet a-gain.
Smite death's threat'ning wave before you; God be with you till we meet a-gain.

CHORUS

Till we meet, ... till we meet, Till we meet at Je - sus' feet;
Till we meet, till we meet, till we meet;

Till we meet, ... till we meet, God be with you till we meet a-gain.
Till we meet, till we meet,

INDEX

TOPICAL INDEX